2

MIX TAPE

EQ-70μs
BIAS-HIGH

Compact Cassette

Made in Japan

RT-60XA

Noise
Reduction

☐ **IN**
☐ **OUT**

C-60

universe

First published in the United States of America in 2004 by
Universe Publishing
A division of Rizzoli International Publications, Inc.
300 Park Avenue South
New York, NY 10010
www.rizzoliusa.com

Text Copyright © 2004 Thurston Moore
Artwork Copyright © 2004 the artists
Printed and bound in China

2007 2008 / 10 9 8 7 6 5 4

ISBN: 978-0-7893-1199-3

Library of Congress Control Number: 2004109184

Rizzoli Editor: Eva Prinz
Concept & design by

the
simultaneous
workshop

mix tape

the art of cassette culture
edited by thurston moore

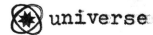 universe

Let us now sing the PRAISES of the MIX TAPE

CONTENTS

introduction

by thurston moore

The first time I'd ever even heard of someone making a mix tape was in 1978. The "Dean of Rock Critics," Robert Christgau, was writing in the *Village Voice* about his favorite Clash record, which just happened to be one he made himself: a tape of all the non–LP b–sides by the band. The Clash made great singles, and they made great LPs, and they would usually put the singles on the LPs but not the b–side of the singles. Anyway, this was a great idea to my rock critic–reading mind. And one aspect really struck me: Mr. Christgau said it was a tape he made to give to friends. He had made his own personalized Clash record and was handing it out as a memento of his rock 'n' roll devotion.

There's one thing he had that I did not: a tape deck. In those days, tape decks were as essential as turntables. And they were as bulky as well. But right around this time Sony issued the Walkman. The Walkman was a portable tape player half the size of a regular portable player—the kind you generally would see on journalists. These new Walkman players were all about hanging off the shoulder with headphones and bopping around the city listening to tunes. I suppose the record industry expected the consumer to buy cassettes of the LPs, and the consumer surely did, but hey—why not buy blank cassettes and record tracks from LPs and play those instead? Of course this is what every Walkman user did, and before long, there were warning stickers on records and cassettes, stating: **HOME TAPING IS KILLING MUSIC!** If anything, it was a quaint forebear to today's industry paranoia over CD-burning and Internet downloading.

I had not the coin for a Walkman in the late '70s or early '80s, but my upstairs neighbor, the artist Dan Graham, had a really nice one—plus he had tons of LPs. He was buying every punk rock and new wave record issued, taping them, and turning me onto tapes which I'd then play on my rag-tag stereo. Around 1980–81, there was a spontaneous scene of young bands issuing singles of super-fast hardcore punk, most of which subscribed to a certain formula of thrash. Bands like Minor Threat, Negative Approach, Necros, Battalion of Saints, Adolescents, Sin 34, The Meatmen, Urban Waste, Void, Crucifucks, Youth Brigade, The Mob, Gang Green, etc., etc. They were great! They were great live and they made really great records. Very on-the-cheap and each tune was hardly a minute long. I was fanatical and bought them all as soon as they came out. I would stop each day at the Rat Cage on Avenue A and buy any new hardcore 7" they'd have on the wall. This,

of course, cost money—but not too much. Each single was only two or three dollars. But I still was just a dishwasher at a Soho restaurant—not exactly raking in the dough—but I needed these sides! My love Kim would come home from work each day, which was either at Todd's Copy Shop on Mott Street or waitressing at Elephant & Castle on Prince Street, and I'd be playing hardcore singles all day. I think she even wrote some lyrics about her boyfriend [me] doing this. I felt slightly guilty, but I also felt I needed to hear these records in a more time-fluid way, and it hit me that I could make a killer mix tape of all the best songs from these records—and since they were all so short and they all had the same kind of sound and energy, the mix tape would be a monolithic hardcore rush. As we had access to Dan's apartment, I went up there and did just that. I made what I thought was the most killer hardcore tape ever. I wrote 'H' on one side, and 'C' on the other. That night, while we were in bed, and after Kim had fallen asleep, I put the cassette on our stereo cassette player, dragged one of the little speakers over to the bed, and listened to the tape at ultra-low thrash volume. I was in a state of humming bliss. This music had every cell and fiber in my body on heavy sizzle mode. It was sweet. For my birthday that summer, Kim bought me a Walkman with a speaker built into it. This allowed me to have the Walkman right next to my pillow and play the 'H/C' mix tape at an even more intimate range. As years roared by, I would make many mix tapes, but I utilized a far broader musical input. I would basically make them just for Kim, and we would play them, lose them, bring them on tour, or lend them out and never see them again.

Before one Sonic Youth tour in the mid-80s, we decided to get a cassette player for the van. One idea was to install a dashboard unit, but that was rather pricey. At the time, there was a street trend in NYC of hip-hop heads blasting rap mix tapes through massive boomboxes, or "ghetto blasters." Hip-hop street style was all about phat-style hugeness. Sneakers were giant with super-wide laces, glasses were as big as half your face, gold chains were called "ropes" because they were so thick and chunky, and portable cassette players were getting to be the size of shopping carts. Knowing this, I immediately appointed myself the band member who would "take care of the tape player" for the van that summer. I went down to this crazy consumer electronics joint on Delancey Street in lower Manhattan, which sold those monster units. Delancey Street, and the adjunct Orchard Street, was the downtown area where all the hip-hop clothes and accessories were sold then. Orchard Street was shop after shop of outdoor racks with the latest Adidas and Fila kicks, vinyl sweatrock pants, deerskin jackets and Kangol hats—all sold by aging

Hasidic Jews. Sunday afternoons were insane on this street, with dudes carting their oversized boomboxes blasting Spoonie G and DST (great old-school rapper, his name stood for Delancey Street). Then there were indie-rocker punkoids like me—hungry and lit-up, weaving through it all. Hip-hop mix tapes, sold on card tables, began to heed to a value system dictated by whomever compiled the tracks. To me, the most interesting ones were the tapes made by rappers who recorded direct to cassette and then duped copies to sell. Between chaos and destitution, I was never of the mind to procure any of these—but I was buying all the rap 12"s I could afford. As Run DMC and LL Cool J were hitting hard, and Def Jam was throwing a new punk rock/hip-hop hybrid into the works, records were being released at a swift clip. This made daily life pretty damn exciting for record hounds like me. Almost any rap 12" could be found in the cut-out bins of Sounds record store on St. Mark's Place, and almost every one was marked .99¢. I made a dozen solid mix tapes of NYC hip-hop and had planned to jam them all summer long in the van on tour. I wasn't sure whether Kim, Lee, and Steve were aware of all these obscure sides, but the music was so raw and current that I was almost positive we'd all be "doing the wop" and break-dancing across the USA. So I went into this Delancey Street store, and, using the band's limited funds, bought the biggest boombox on display. It was massive (It *is* massive! I still have it). We all met in front of our rehearsal space on East 4th Street between Avenue A and B at about 10 a.m. to pack the gear and head on out. When I arrived, everyone looked at the blaster and was astounded that I had blown band money on this unwieldy hunk of plastic. I told them it didn't cost much for what it was: two decks, AM/FM radio, and full on shortwave reception. Plus, it had sick lights which moved while songs played, *and* it had an alarm that could be set off if anyone ever touched it—and the alarm was crazy loud. But design functionality was problematic, as there really wasn't that much room in the van after the band and the equipment was loaded. The boombox was almost like an extra body, about the size of a small kid. My solution was to place it between the two front seats and have it stand on end, where it would face the back. This actually kind of worked and placated everyone. As we drove through the Holland Tunnel and began to distance ourselves from the city, I thought it might be an OK time to throw a tape on. I jammed in the first of the compiled rap tapes, and the boombox sounded superb. Cheap, but superb. And funky. The music could only sound this good coming through this kind of system. Within 20 seconds of playback, dissent came drifting forward, "Can you turn it down please?," "What other tapes did you bring?," "I got some Johnny Cash...". By the time we hit the West Coast, we were comfortable with the Conion (that was the brand name—we nicknamed it "the Conan"). We would have it onstage with us when we played, and I would mic it through the PA for between-song tape action. Kids would give us cassettes all across America—some of them hopeful demos, and some of them mix tapes, and we'd jam them all. The Conan takes 16 size "D" batteries, but it also has an AC extension cord. It still has all the rock 'n' roll stickers on it from Meat Puppets to Killdozer. By tour's end, there must have been hundreds of tapes strewn about the van, with plastic cases stomped and cracked.

Years later I would make a box of mix tapes for Kim when she went to the hospital to have our baby. I still see them floating around sometimes as I run through the detritus of our household, and, like a photo, I flash to that amazing time. While preparing this book, almost every person I solicited had a tale to tell about the mix tapes they had made for themselves or others, and ones they received in return. And almost every person bemoaned the fact that their beloved tapes had vanished. So many people had talked about the beautiful and wild cassette cover art adorning their tapes. Some, like myself, never did this. It was the simple listing of the artists and the song titles which held the magic. CD technology displaced the cassette in the mainstream, and it is just recently that mix CDs have become a new cultural love letter/trading-post.

This book can only represent one zillionth of the people out there who have made the coolest tapes for themselves or others. In that respect, it simply exists as a nod to the true love and ego involved in sharing music with friends and lovers. Trying to control sharing through music is like trying to control an affair of the heart—nothing will stop it.

Thurston Moore

Here, let me play you something.

Listen. Are you listening?
Back in the '80s, at a dinner party uptown, I remember Michael Gira of Swans playing some of his new material.

At this time Swans were huge—the sound of each song was more bodybusting than the last. We complied and honored Michael's wish to absorb this new pounding rock whomp. It was soul-searing, and he wanted us to honor it by paying attention. We did, and it was great, but Lydia Lunch was kind of loudly discussing something with Kim on the couch. I could tell Michael was getting slightly perturbed by Lydia's partial concentration. We all know that feeling you want to share something, particularly something of your own creation with your friends, and there may be somebody there only halfway paying attention, and it bugs you because they need to get the whole story or it will be trite, and God forbid your work be anything trite.

In the early '70s film *Lipstick*, an avant-garde composer attempts to play his music for a fetching Mariel Hemingway, but her phone keeps ringing, and she goes off to chat. Enraged by her non-committance, he attacks her. Consequently, this makes the only cinematic portrayal of an avant-garde musician as a serial psycho.

Michael said—with clipped tone through an intense smile—"Lydia!"

Lydia: "What, Mike?"

Michael, gesturing at stereo: "Listen."

Lydia, in an inimitable Lydia Lunch comeback snarl: "I can't help but *not* to."

Which begs the question: are you listening, or just hearing? There is a difference, of course. We all learned that in grade school, while the teachers droned on and we gazed elsewhere, hearing the linguic buzz but listening to something else: the mix tape mind.

T.M.

777

I GARASJE HELVETE

La Fiancée du Vampire

I Garasje Helvete (In Garage Hell). This tape was given to me by Kjell Runar "Killer" Jenssen after I asked him about '60s punk and garage rock. Kjell Runar is a walking music encyclopedia and has one of the biggest record collections of anyone I know, and he's more than willing to share his knowledge. So he dug in there and put together this tape for me. The only track I could remember having heard before was "Surfin' Bird" by The Trashmen, burned into my memory when seeing the "singing asshole" sequence in John Waters' *Pink Flamingos* on video at age 15.

Lasse Marhaug

"I got a New Zealand noise mix tape from Fredrik, a '60s garage punk tape from Killer, a heavy metal tape from a friend who suffers from serious depression, etc.—all handmade & nice."

SideA: "Høyere enn månen"

N.R. ☐ YES ☐ NO

POSITION NORMAL

maxell

It's a sickness, really, this compiling.

Since I was wee, I have felt to be an arbiter of mood through the sequential playing of organized sound. As little more than a lad, I'd turn the new hi-fi speakers my Old Man was so proud of inward and dangle the lo-fi mic between the grills, capturing the songs I was currently enamored of, dutifully hitting the pause button on the tape recorder on the tail end of the fade out.

When I barely graduated from high school, the Old Man gave me a choice: He would either pay for college, or give me a thousand dollars cash for a new fuck-all stereo of my very own. One guess which way I went on that one. In retrospect, I'm sure I was brutally ripped off by the blow-dried moustache I bought the thing from, but damn if it wasn't the best grand I ever blew.

Bolstered by a dead-end gig at the local used record store, I amassed a massive collection of vinyl, which I dissected over and over, laying the pieces end to end on magnetic tape. These were the purest moments of the affliction, constructing my own private radio station, one that could match my teenage psychosis riff for riff, made for no other consumption than mine.

Soon, though, I discovered that one's musical tastes could be used to unlock the holiest of holy places: what lived beneath the Jordache jeans of whatever unsuspecting girl I played sensitive for. And so it has been ever since—me, carefully constructing the sets to achieve the desired effect—be it salacious or self-absorbed. Now, that being said, I give you a mix that will open your eyes to the simple truth that says: all you have to do to live like a rock star is know which rock stars to like.

Pat Griffin

The One That I Am Currently Puttting On For The Ladies
20th Century Boy—T Rex
Cowboys—Portishead (live at Roseland, NYC)
Slave—The Stones
One Gun Salute—Roy Ayers
Criminal—Fiona Apple
Sexy MF—Prince
Ray of Light—Madonna
Sidewalk Serfer Girl—Super Furry Animals
Protection—Massive Attack featuring Tracy Thorn
You Win Again—Jerry Lee Lewis
7 Bridges Road—Dolly Parton
Cowgirl In The Sand—Neil Young
Lovin Machine—Jon Spencer Blues Explosion
Everything Is Everything—Lauryn Hill
Lovin' Touchin' Squeezin'—Journey
Jelly Bread—Booker T and the MG's
A Little Sugar In My Bowl—Nina Simone
Let Down—Radiohead
Tupelo Honey—Van Morrison
Danke Schoen—Wayne Newton

WARNING

SENSITIVE PUSSIES SHOULD NOT LISTEN TO THIS AWESOME SET OF DITTIES.

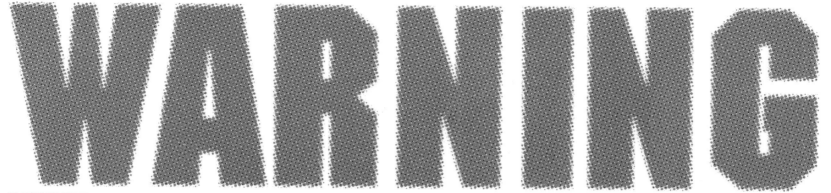

This mix is filled with the power of rock and is fueled by Satan himself. If you dare to listen to the fine music I have assembled, you'll instantly be transported back to a time and place where people snorted coke off Nagel paintings, and leopard–print spandex camel–toes gave young boys instant erections. A time when wearing blue eye shadow and leg warmer socks was the bee's knees, and corndogs filled the guts of many a fine hard–rockin' American teen. Rock music never left my soul, and fuckwits who are addicted to lame-ass, ghetto–fabulous, sampled, dogshit rap music have ruined it for the hesher whom I believe lives in us all.

Long live rock 'n' roll!

Ahmet Zappa

LICK IT UP — KISS
SHAKE ME — CINDERELLA
I BELIEVE IN MIRACLES — RAMONES
VOODOO — BLACK SABBATH
LET ME PUT MY LOVE INTO YOU —
MR. BROWNSTONE — AC/DC
THE WIDOWMAKER — WIDOWMAKER GUNS 'N' ROSES
HE'S A WHORE — CHEAP TRICK
I'LL WAIT — VAN HALEN
GOODBYE TO ROMANCE — OZZY
SMOOTH IT UP IN YA — BULLET BOYS
LOOKS THAT KILL — MÖTLEY CRÜE
SHE'S AN ANGEL — LOVE/HATE
FINGER ON THE TRIGGER — ENUFF Z'NUFF
DENIM + LEATHER — SAXON
BIG CITY NIGHTS — SCORPIONS
CAN'T WAIT — FOREIGNER
STILL OF THE NIGHT — WHITESNAKE

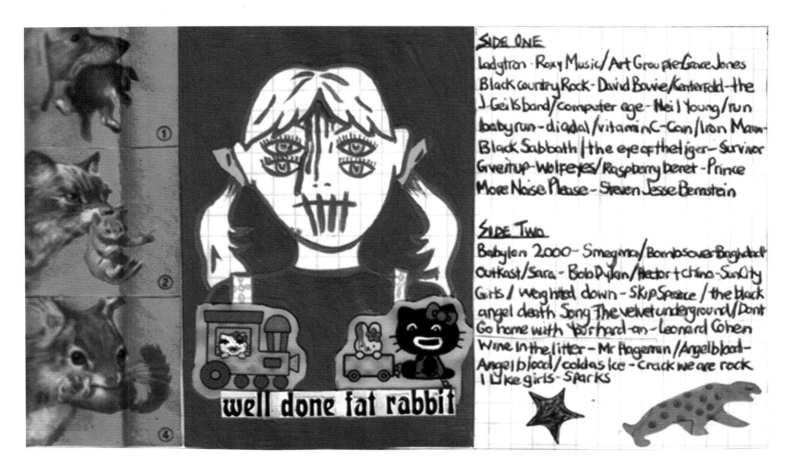

Here's a tape I did for an ex-Polly Shang Kuan Band member. I never gave her it because I had a fight with her boyfriend 'cause he's an asshole. Then she sent a note to us saying we can't be friends anymore. Boofuckinghoo. So she didn't get the tape. She's a loser anyway.

Karen Lollypop

FOR: MIKE WATT ENJOY!
FROM: STEVEN DROZD

1. WASP - BLACK SABBATH
2. KNIFE-EDGE - ELP
3. IT'S A BIT OF PAIN - FAUST
4. WICHITA LINEMAN - GLEN CAMPBELL
5. MEETING OF THE SPIRITS - MAHAVISHNU ORCHESTRA
6. EXPECTING to FLY - NEIL YOUNG
7. GALILEO - MICE PARADE / 8. SAETA - MILES DAVIS
9. JACKIE BLUE - OZARK MOUNTAIN DAREDEVILS
10. AT LAST I AM FREE - ROBERT WYATT
11. CITADEL - ROLLING STONES
12. PLAN B PART 2 - the PARIS GUN
13. OSCILLATIONS - SILVER APPLES
14. LOSING TOUCH with MY MIND - SPACEMEN 3
15. AFTER the FLOOD - TALK TALK
16. COLTRANE LOOP - STEVEN for DR. WATT

For my friend Elizabeth Hahn I made a mix of some live stuff of The Black Gang—the final version that toured with me—that had me on bass and spiel, Nels Cline on guitar and Bob Lee on drums. She's seen me play a bunch (even with this lineup) but I wanted her to be able to have some to listen back to and to think of me. I love giving her documents. She also turned me on to Marcia Ball, a pianist from Texas (Elizabeth plays piano too). I ended up making three mixes—I just put the songs into sequences that made sense to me. I tried to make little rivers, with both the words and music. It was trippy because I had never heard of her before, and it was all new, so I had no preconceptions. The only thing I had in mind was what I knew about Elizabeth as a person.

The guitarist from The Flaming Lips, Steve Drozd, just gave me a mix. It's pretty righteous. He said he was thinking of me. He's quite cool peeps and has a good heart.

Mike Watt

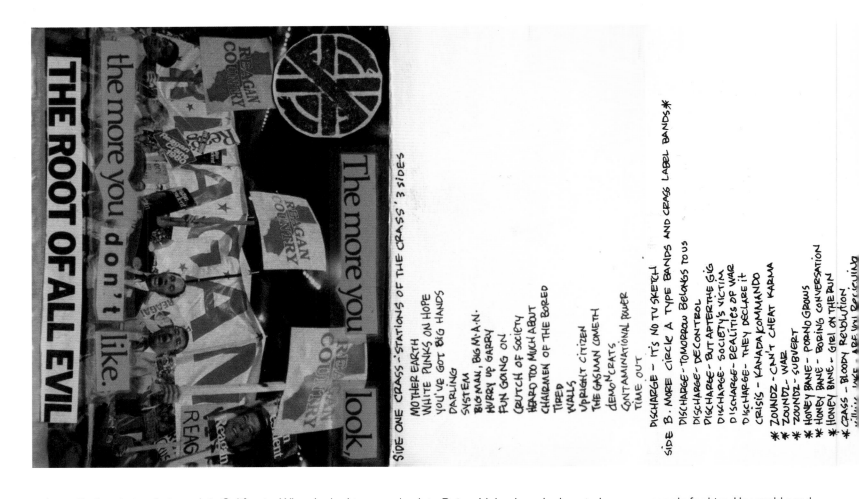

THE ROOT OF ALL EVIL

the more you don't like.

the more you look,

The more you look,

SIDE ONE CRASS - STATIONS OF THE CRASS 3 SIDES

MOTHER EARTH
WHITE PUNKS ON HOPE
YOU'VE GOT BIG HANDS
DARLING
SYSTEM
BIG MAN, BIG M·A·N·
HURRY UP GARRY
FUN GOING ON
CRUTCH OF SOCIETY
HEARD TOO MUCH ABOUT
CHAIRMEN OF THE BORED
TIRED
WALLS
UPRIGHT CITIZEN
THE GASMAN COMETH
DEMONCRATS
CONTAMINATIONAL POWER
TIME OUT

SIDE B. MORE CIRCLE A TYPE BANDS AND CRASS LABEL BANDS *

DISCHARGE - IT'S NO TV SKETCH
DISCHARGE - TOMORROW BELONGS TO US
DISCHARGE - DECONTROL
DISCHARGE - BUT AFTER THE GIG
DISCHARGE - SOCIETY'S VICTIM
DISCHARGE - REALITIES OF WAR
DISCHARGE - THEY DECLARE IT
CRISIS - KANADA KOMMANDO
* ZOUNDZ - CAN'T CHEAT KARMA
* ZOUNDZ - WAR
* ZOUNDZ - SUBVERT
* HONEY BANE - PORNO GROWS
* HONEY BANE - BORING CONVERSATION
* HONEY BANE - GIRL ON THE RUN
* CRASS - BLOODY REVOLUTION

I met Pushead at a skate park in California. When he had to move back to Boise, Idaho, he asked me to buy new records for him. He would send me a list and cash and I would go to record stores in Los Angeles and buy records he couldn't find in Boise. To show his appreciation he made me these compilations. I've kept them for over 20 years.

Glen E. Friedman

23

SIDE 2 2.14.82 DOLBY   31 SONGS
  BLACK FLAG - MACHINE
  BLACK FLAG - LIFE OF PAIN
  FUNERAL - POLITICANS ARE SICK
  VAPUKERS - PROTEST + SURVIVE
  CIRCLE ONE - DESTROY EXXON
  TOXIC REASONS - RIOT SQUAD
  SOCIETY DOG - THE BABY IS DEAD
  BLITZ - 45 REVELUTIONS
  GBH - NO SURVIVORS
  FARTZ - YOU'VE GOT A BRAIN
  SUMBHUMANS - SOCIETY
  SUBHUMANS - WHO'S GONNA FIGHT
  SOA - LOST IN SPACE
  DISTORTION - ACTION MAN
  STAINS - SICK + CRAZY
  DISORDER - COMPLETE DISORDER
  EFFIGIES - STRONG BOX
  CIRCLE ONE - FUCK OFF
 CIVIL DISOBENIENCE - CAMPAIGN PROMISES
  INSANE - DEAD + GONE
  NECROS - BAD DREAM
  NECROS - PAST COMES BACK TO HAUNT ME
  NECROS - REJECT
  FARTZ - CON GAME
  MEATMEN - MEATMEN STOMP
  KRAUT - LAST CHANCE
  NEGATIVE APPROACH - LOST CAUSE
  VAPUKERS - NEVER AGAIN
  MINORTHREAT - FILLER
  LAW + ORDER - POWER
  McDONALD'S - MINUPATURE GOLF

  — PLAY LOUD, SO YOU DON'T HEAR THE
  SIRENS, DON'T HEAR THE HORNS, DON'T HEAR
  THE PEOPLE, DON'T HEAR THE WORLD AND EYE.

67 BLOOD SPLATTERING DICK PIERCING HITS!
IF YOU WANTED BLAQD STAB YOUR FRIENDLY
GARDENER!....

THE GREAT LOST Ex NITRO EXPLOSION OF BRAIN BLISTERING SONIC
ATTACKS FOR TOTAL MASS ANNILATION BEYOND HUMAN CRANIUM
COMBUSTION OR THE FUCKING GNARLIEST SAMPLER EVER MADE..

Hardcore reality

HORRIBLE

SIDE A 2.14.82 DOLBY   36 SONGS
STRIKE UNDER - FUCKING UNIFORMS
NECROS - IQ 32
NECROS - YOUTH CAMP
MINOR THREAT - BOTTLED VIOLENCE
INSANE - POLITICS
DESCENDENTS - GLOBAL PROBING
SOCIAL UNREST - MAKING ROOM FOR YOUTH
SOCIAL UNREST - JOIN THE PEOPLE
DISCHARGE - IT'S NO T.V. SKETCH
YOUTH PATROL - AMERICAS POWER
ABRASIVE WHEELS - VICIOUS CIRCLE
BLACK FLAG - CLOCKED IN
GBH - FREAK
EFFIGIES - GUNS OR BALLOTS
SUBHUMANZ - DRUGS OF YOUTH
FARTZ - CAMPAIGN SPEECH
YOUTH BRIGADE - FULL SPEED AHEAD
DISORDER - DAILY LIFE
TEEN IDLES - SNEAKERS
MEAT PUPPETS - FOREIGN LAWNS
GOVERNMENT ISSUE - RELIGIOUS RIPOFF
PARTISANS - POLICE STORY
BAD RELIGION - SLAVES
THE FIX - NO IDOLS
VARUKERS - NO SCAPEGOAT
SECRET HATE - NEW ROUTINE
SECRET HATE - SUICIDE
MINOR THREAT - GUILTY OF BEING WHITE
POLITICAL CRAP - SLOW DEATH
NECROS - PEER PRESSURE
NECROS - RACE RIOT
NECROS - WAR GAME
DISCHARGE - AIN'T NO FEEBLE BASTARD
DESCENDENTS - I LIKE FOOD
DESCENDENTS - WEINER STINZEL
LAW + ORDER - CRITIC'S CHOICE

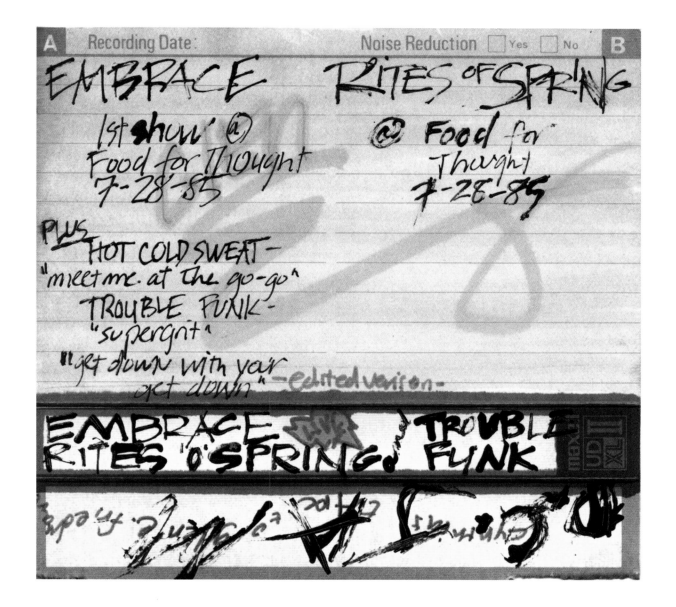

Cynthia Connolly

IN THE FUTURE, WHEN SOCIAL SCIENTISTS STUDY THE MIX TAPE PHENOMENON, THEY WILL CONCLUDE—IN FANCY LANGUAGE—THAT THE MIX TAPE WAS A FORM OF "SPEECH" PARTICULAR TO THE LATE TWENTIETH CENTURY, SOON REPLACED BY THE "PLAY LIST."

It takes time and effort to put a mix tape together. The time spent implies an emotional connection with the recipient. It might be a desire to go to bed, or to share ideas. The message of the tape might be: *I love you. I think about you all the time. Listen to how I feel about you.* Or, maybe: *I love me. I am a tasteful person who listens to tasty things. This tape tells you all about me.* There is something narcissistic about making someone a tape, and the act of giving the tape puts the recipient in our debt somewhat. Like all gifts, the mix

tape comes with strings attached. I haven't made a lot of mix tapes in my life, but I made at least a couple in the summer of 1987, one for my former and then future girlfriend, and one for my friends Damon Krukowski and Naomi Yang, right when we were putting together our rock band, Galaxie 500.

I can't remember what I put on the tape for my girlfriend, although I'm certain I included "Back In Your Life" and "Affection" by Jonathan Richman. Because I wanted to be back in her life, and I wanted her to not be such a chicken and show me some affection. Which she ultimately did, though not until I left town.

Luckily, Damon and Naomi kept the cassette that I made for them. It is titled "The Tape That Dean Made One Night." Looking over the track listing on this tape is like reading an old diary entry, and I was taken back to my life in 1987.

I was living on Front Street in New York City, about 50 feet from the Brooklyn Bridge. My girlfriend had told me she just wanted to be friends, and that I was too demanding. I was feeling pretty sorry for myself. I listened to Jonathan Richman and Moe Tucker and the 13th Floor Elevators and Big Star and Ed Kuepper's fantastic and sad album *Electrical Storm*. And I worked at boring temp jobs, doing typing and word processing. Damon and Naomi came to town for the summer, and we started to play music together in a room at my parents' house. Being that I had no real job and no girlfriend, I decided to move to Cambridge and work other boring temp jobs and be in a band.

Starting a band with your friends is a little like falling in love. You spend all your time together. You have so many things you want to tell each other. Hence the tape. When I look at the cassette today, I see that it is almost a recipe of ingre-dients for Galaxie 500. Some of our very favorite artists are included. There is Moe Tucker, whose gig I attended in 1987 at TT the Bear's Place in Cambridge. The Pixies were opening for her; I didn't like them. I stayed on Damon and Naomi's sofa that night, and somehow I managed to do an interview with Moe and Jad Fair the next morning, posing as a rock critic.

We loved The Dream Syndicate and other bands who were sometimes called the "Paisley Underground"—particularly The Rain Parade, Opal, and The Salvation Army, who I had seen at Storyville in Kendall Square. I had seen Pere Ubu in 1980 at Irving Plaza in New York; then again, tripping on mushrooms, in 1981; and yet again when they reformed in 1987. Damon and Naomi and I went together to see them perform at Nightstage in Cambridge. They had two drummers, Scott Krauss, who played with shoes, and Chris Cutler, who played barefoot. We also saw Jonathan Richman at Nightstage, right after our first album *Today* was released. We were thrilled that we got to go backstage and give him a copy of the LP, and he talked to us about how he came to record "Don't Let Our Youth Go To Waste."

Shockabilly are represented here by three tracks; they are one of my favorite bands of the '80s. I had seen them play at 8BC in New York in 1985 (when 8th Street between B and C looked like a war zone), they would throw stuff at each other on stage. Galaxie 500 and Shockabilly have little in common, but their bassist, Kramer, was to be an important force in our lives. It was the Half Japanese record he produced that prompted me to call him one day to see if we would produce our band.

The Modern Lovers were my favorite long-extinct Boston band, and Mission of Burma were my favorite recently disbanded one. I saw them once, playing an antiwar rally in Harvard Yard (the war in El Salvador and Nicaragua). Like Galaxie 500, Mission of Burma were not hugely popular in their hometown.

I also included the Joy Division 7" flexidisk "Komakino/Incubation"—not their best songs, but I thought everything they did was great. Joy Division bassist Peter Hook's simple and melodic playing style was an influence on Naomi. We all got to meet Peter Hook one day, too—he came to see us play in Manchester.

The one thing that amazes me about this tape is that I've been lucky enough to meet a lot of the musicians who appear on it: Jonathan Richman, Shockabilly, Moe Tucker, Steve Wynn of the Dream Syndicate, Robyn Hitchcock (he joined Galaxie 500 on stage for a version of the Beatles'

"Rain"), Peter Hook, David Thomas of Pere Ubu, and the members of Mission of Burma also. Perhaps in the making of this tape I summoned those people to me. It kind of looks that way.

Another band that I discovered in 1987 and shared with Damon and Naomi was the Spacemen 3. This year I received a great cassette in the mail from the Spacemen's Pete Kember, as we developed a friendship and made a record together. His tape included "Lili Marlene" by Marlene Dietrich, with Burt Bacharach's orchestra, "Sun Arise" by Rolf Harris (whose strange television show I watched as a child—he is perhaps best known for "Tie Me Kangaroo Down, Sport"), a soaring version of "Perfidia" by Xavier Cugat, "Love Is Strange" by Bob and Sylvia, some great Animals tunes I had never heard, from their LP *Animalization*, "She's Coming Home" by the Wailers (US), and "Time Will Tell" by Bob Marley and the Wailers. Pete has compiled some of these same songs for a CD released by the Spanish label Munster Records, under the title *Spacelines*. My hope is that Pete's tape will summon the spirits of Marlene Dietrich and Rolf Harris.

Dean Wareham

Dean made us this tape just as we were starting Galaxie 500 together, in 1987, and we listened to it a lot at the time. It's like a little time capsule of musical influences at a particular moment.

Naomi Yang

If you cut random bits of this tape together, you'd probably come up with an alternate version of the first Galaxie 500 album.

Damon Krukowski

disc 1
1. into the chaser portland, or.
2. everyday- atp festival LA
3. ella's incredible floating sound machine atp festival LA
4. fantasy hay co -op - atp festival
5. breakdown portland, or.
6. evaporator- salem, or.
7. revolution sk-1- salem, or.

disc 2
1. aircom uk
2. jill's thump
3. extension
4. patti lama
5. in between
6. 2nd ave. (reprise)
7. vindiloo

I2RO italy
usa
West Coast
RABAT Morocco
FYA France
HBL Switzerland
YV1BC Venezuela
VK3ME Australia
DJA 2002
termite club leeds, uk
2000
HJ2A Colombi
RV59 Russia
W2XE New York
TIUI Madagasca

po box 74141 vancouver BC   V5V 5C8 canada

all songs p+c 2002 ghetto music

MUSIC'S GOLDEN STREAM FLOODS THE ETHER

U : SOUND

friends wingtip slant. my favorite mix
tape came from Jackie Dustdevils. most
great Royal Trux indie 7 inches combined
perfectly. The Fall encapsulating swell maps
that summer tall dwarves perfectly... it
was tied Let "Katches" so Vasalines Brian
perfect we started Bobann
honory Red Crayaia And sucked.
played **2222**

ELMERS ASST COMIC HEARTS 3OZ.
656769

OL55
N47

65676
OL55
N47

SECTION
98

SLOT
S0001

CASE:

267

Rex _13 The silk incredible string band big huge LP.
St Coast Pop Art experimental band.

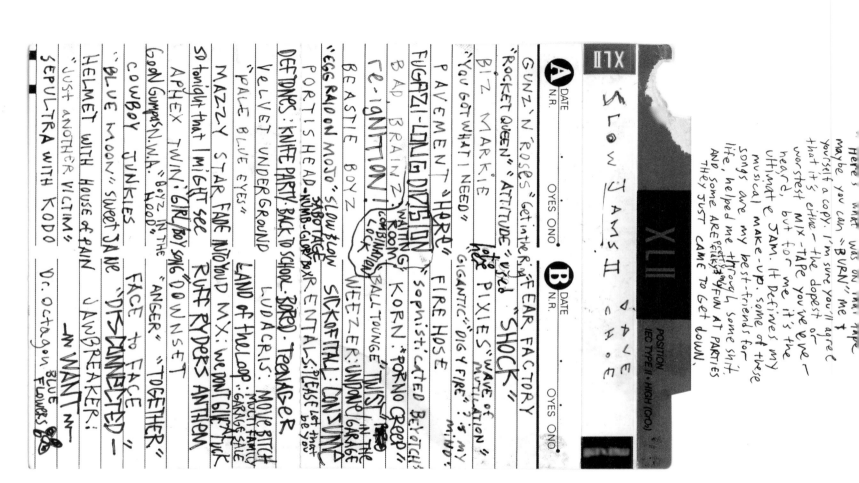

David Choe

The mix tape as a form of AMERICAN FOLK ART:

predigested cultural artifacts combined with homespun technology and magic markers turn the mix tape to a message in a bottle. I am no mere consumer of pop culture, it says, but also a producer of it. Mix tapes mark the moment of consumer culture in which listeners attained control over what they heard, in what order and at what cost. It liberated us from music stores and radios in the same way radios and recordings liberated generations earlier from the need to be present at the performance of live music.

THE PATHETIC:

THEY ARE PATHETIC, NO MATTER WHAT. SOMETHING IS LOST. IS IT OUR INNOCENCE? LIKE ALL FOLK ART, AN ATTEMPT TO RECAPTURE LOST **INNOCENCE**

The mix tape is a list of quotations, a poetic form in fact: the cento is a poem made up of lines pulled from other poems. The new poet collects and remixes. Similarly an operation of taste, it is also cousin to the curious passion of the obsessive collector. Unable to express himself in a "pure" art, the collector finds himself in obsessive acquisition. Collecting is strangely hot and cold, passionate and calculating. All we can agree upon is that it's not the same thing as making art. Or is it? A mix tape can never be perfect. My taste as a mixer tells you even more about me than my taste as a consumer already does. No mix tape is accidental.

They are avant-garde too, like the cut-up. A parallel to Xerox art, an antecedent to sampling. The mix cassette as a situation-ist spectacle, a derive. Making the existing world tell tales it does not intend to tell. You get the world to send you a message it never meant to send.

My friend David Burns' mix tape. As a CD of 8–track hits, it skips a technological generation, a strange act of incest. Being a decade younger than me, the pop hits of the '70s were mysteriously potent to him, while in me they invoke a faint queasiness epitomized in the music of Wayne Newton. To him, this music was nostalgic, while I remembered a sleepless night on a bus trip from Paris to Athens solely accompanied by one endless 8-track of Tom Jones' greatest hits. The two drivers would switch places in mid-road, leaping up in a parody of Greek table dancing while the other scooted in to the shriek of "What's new pussycat? Meeow! Meow, meow-meow!"

Note: Many of these songs are covers from the original recordings which were very popular in the MUZAK 1970 8-track era. In order to replicate the 8-track experience, David had to record the irritating CLACK as the low-res cartridge switched from track to track. This noise was then digitized and spliced in every two or three songs to capture the discrete charm of the 8-track experience.

1. Green Green, The New Christie Minstrels
2. Deep Purple, Donny and Marie Osmond
3. Calcutta, Lawrence Welk
4. Cherry Cherry, Neil Diamond
5. Delta Dawn, Helen Reddy
6. Snow Bird, Anne Murray
7. Tie A Yellow Ribbon, Tony Orlando and Dawn
8. Gentle On My Mind, Glenn Campbell
9. Raindrops Keep Falling On My Head, BJ Thomas
10. Daydream Believer, Anne Murray
11. Mrs. Robinson, The Ray Conniff Singers
12. What A Day For A Daydream, Lovin' Spoonful
13. Tiny Bubbles, Don Ho
14. You'll Never Get To Heaven, Burt Bacharach and Dionne Warwick
15. Solitaire, The Carpenters
16. You Needed Me, Anne Murray
17. Solitary Man, Neil Diamond
18. Up Up And Away, The Ray Conniff Singers
19. Spinning Wheel, Blood, Sweat and Tears
20. Charade, Henry Mancini
21. End Credits Song to the Donny and Marie Show

Matias Viegener

Bloot–O. Snug. Margarine Hoot. What A Wonderful Doughnut. Tape for Grey. Gal Punk.

With titles like these, what could the recipient's heart do but melt? And the contents... Screaming Trees to Tall Dwarfs to Barbara Manning to Boss Hog to Pearls Before Swine to Flesh Eaters to Psycho Daisies to Roy Harper...

I'd slot these in at work, crank the volume, and be surrounded with Byron's tesseract world view and cranked humor. It was a shared alternate plane that kept me with him, even as I navigated the channels of the corporate nerd world—my tether to the world I really loved. The tapes are stretched to the point that the original beats droop and hop in odd syncopations, but when they're on the box I am back with Byron and the Psycho Daisies in those halcyon cyclonic days, just "Walkin 'round on my rubber legs-unh-Ahm feelin' great cuz I'm trippin around..."

Lili Dwight

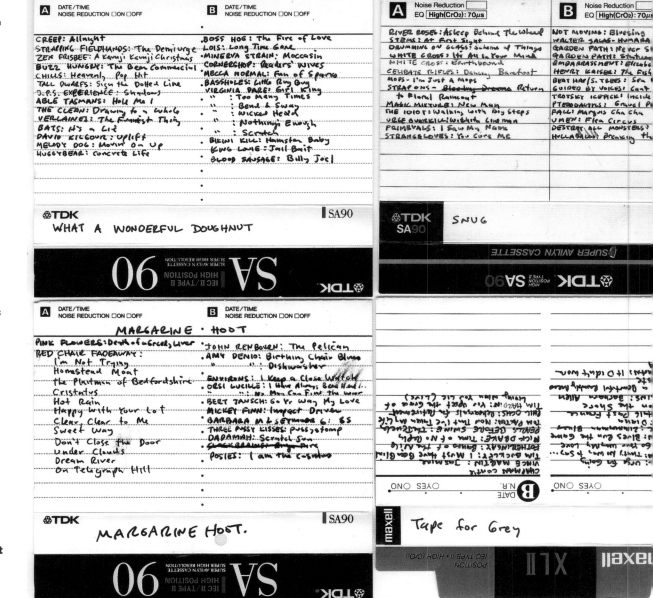

Don't Take My Word For It is the name of one of many elaborate mix tapes made for me back in college (oh the '80s—the decade of the mix tape!) by Jonathan Marx (founding member of the band Lambchop), from Nashville, but we were living in New York City at the time, which facilitated our record-buying habit. While we both collected music pretty obsessively, Jonathan was always introducing me to wild shit I had no idea about (in this case, The Homosexuals, The Boys, and The Delmore Brothers, among others), and pairing it with seemingly incongruous other music, but it all worked. My band, Superchunk, ended up covering a Flys song on our first single, a song I first heard on one of Jonathan's tapes. Jonathan was quite into the cut-and-paste aesthetic and instead of just filling out the given tracklist card, he glued Xeroxed photographs directly to every available surface—insides and outsides of the box, the tape itself, etc. I think this tape dates to 1987.

Mac McCaughan

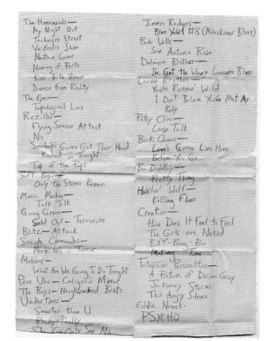

Winding over San Francisco's Twin Peaks in my '87 Dodge Aries Wagon, panoramic view to die for, I crank up the volume on Aaron's mix, and Leonard Cohen growls. When he made me this mix, Aaron pulled together tracks that would appeal to a person who listens to Cat Power and Nick Cave, since I apparently once mentioned liking them. For Aaron, when two people are into the same bands, they share a profound connection. Music is important in Aaron's writing—it inspires him, and he weaves song lyrics throughout his manuscripts. Like many other 24-year-olds, he writes about drugs and sexual desire. In his mix, I recognize the scathing intelligence and humor I enjoy in his writing, the same uneasy shifting between alienation and romanticism. But the two older (maternal?) figures on the cover make me nervous. Gladys Presley appears to be being strangled and the other woman, the one with the sledgehammer, has been energetically crossed out with red. These women wouldn't like Cat Power, I tell myself—they can't be me.

Dodie Bellamy

1. "untitled"—Interpol
2. jj72 - "Black Eyed Dog"
3. Bright Eyes "Poison Oak"
4. Leonard Cohen "Famous Blue Raincoa[t]
5. Johnny Cash "The Man Comes Around"
6. Nico "Janitor of Lunacy"
7. Bauhaus "She's In Parties"
8. Roxy Music "In Every Dream Home a Heartache"
9. Antony and The Johnsons - "Soft Black Sta[r]
10. Tom Waits "Innocent When You Drea[m]
11. Boys Next Door "Shivers"
12. Nancy Sinatra / Lee Hazelwood "San[
13. The Smiths "Sweet and Tender Hooligan"
14. Belle & Sebastian - "She's Losing I[t]
15. David Bowie "Life on Mars?"
16. Siouxsie & The Banshees "Icon"
17. Current Ninety Three "Sleep Has His House

(tracks 3 and 17 live recordings)

8.27.03

XLII·S WILLIE'S MAGICAL MUSIC ROMANCE PART **IV** maxell

A DATE . .
N.R.   ○YES ○NO

ALBERT AYLER - 4 MOST -
DUDU DA PASSIRA - LES McCANN -
OAKLAND ELEMENTARY SCHOOL -
RAY BARRETTO - SHARP FIVE -
AKINA SHŌKICHI - CONFUSE -
LOS VAN VAN - DICK DALE -
JON - ZIMBU TRIO -

B DATE . .
N.R.   ○YES ○NO

CACHAO - GEORGE BRAITH -
EDDIE + THE SHOWMEN - ZIMBO3 -
BLOODSUCKER - LIM DONKRARMT -
RUBALCABA - SATO MASARU -
ROLAND KIRK (SOLO)

Yo THURSTON.
Here's a personal
mixed TAPe FROM
ZORN. ITs a
good one!
Love
Willie

LOVE

love to love you baby
love comes in spurts
love grows where my rosemary goes
love is all around
love is all you need
love-itis
love shack
where is the love?
hey love
I love her all the time
love and other games
love goes to building on fire
love is a battlefield
let's talk about love
my love
one love
I believe in a thing called love
gimme some lovin'
love is for sops
so much in love
love don't live here anymore
addicted to love

(&EGO)

The incredible, beautiful, God–forsaken New York Dolls song "Lookin' For A Kiss" is a track classic to any lovers' mix tape. It would seem first and foremost that LOVE, the emotion, is the key song signifier for any personal love note mix tape. The toughest cowpoke can express his gooey love vibe without losing an iota of man-stench, just by flowing his babe a mix tape with any sweet beat from the Shangri-Las to Whitehouse. One young dude on the great Internet mix tape site artofthemix.org has a tape entitled *You Best Believe I'm In Love (L-U-V)* with nothing but New York Dolls expousing said sentiment. That's one way to drive your love interest batty, unless that person was waaay into the Dolls. And if that's the case, then hey—what's the point of wooing a non-Dolls enthusiast anyhow! In this respect, mix tapes are like matchmaker forms. But why must your match have to be so like yourself—do you just pretty much love yourself? I asked one mix tape maker this question (he's in this book, but would like to remain incognito in light of this). He claims that when making mix tapes, love songs included, they are pretty much for himself first. Sure, he will pass them on to his amour for a Valentine, but he primarily made it because it's the music that kicks his own ass. Is there a desire to convert your lover into you? Why not make a mix tape with songs you know your darling likes, regardless of your own tastes (see Mike Watts' mix tape, he did this— possibly he's the über-male?). With that in mind, "Love The One You're With" takes on a whole new resonance!

T.M.

side one
guernica—panorama view
laurie styvers—beat the reaper
bill fay—'til the christ comes back
sandy denny—next time around
mick softley—i'm so confused
alan hull—one more bottle of wine
david ackles—i've been loved
swingle singers—largo
henske + yester—rapture
neil young—ambulance blues

side two
mike mcgear—woman
michael nesmith—you are the one
claudio rocchi—il melle della api
judee sill—the kiss
randy newman—davy the fatboy
jack nitzsche—last dance
bridget st. john— ask me no questi
roy harper—when an old cricketer
leaves the crease

There was a mix tape I made when I was 15, I believe in order to get a girl to like me, because that is generally why you make mix tapes when you're 15. I had a tape deck that allowed you to record left and right channels separately, so I played dueling DJs, debating the merits of each track and informing my other self of its importance, lineage, and general all-around alreet-ness. I was into words like that then. I don't know what happened to that tape, it's gone, like the two of me that were on that tape. While the tape was a minor success I had an itch-ing feeling I had made a grave error. Later, I realized I had compro-mised myself by putting a The The track on there, because she liked them. I did not, and to this day, I wish I could go back and replace that track. I still remember this misstep vividly. I wasn't true to myself, and as much as the tape was filled with my chattering, my enthusiasm, my soda-fueled proselytizing, it still rang as hollow as the empty cans beside me. So, I'm taking this chance to say sorry, to me. Her? It was her favorite track.

Jim O'Rourke

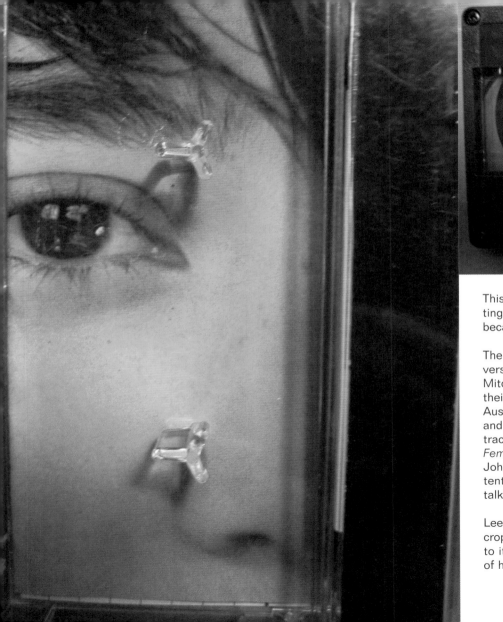

HERE

This is one of the first tapes Lee gave me. We were just getting to know each other, a good time to exchange mixed tapes because it's such a powerful way to reveal who you are.

The tape exemplifies who Lee Ranaldo is. It includes taped conversations of his family on Christmas Eve, with songs by Joni Mitchell and Dylan. There's an interview of Sonic Youth from their 1989 Russian tour and later a goofy session at an Australian radio studio. Nick Cave croons "The Mercy Seat" and Tom Waits belts out "Jersey Girl." The Beach Boys, soundtrack dialogue from Kerouac's *Pull My Daisy* and Godard's *Une Femme est une Femme*, Buddy Holly, The Band, Daniel Johnston, and Henry Cowell all get time on this cassette. The tentative confidence of Thom's voice, Lee's old pal, is heard talking about friendship, love, and the here and now.

Lee simply taped the word HERE on the cassette and used a cropped magazine photo of a boy's face as the cover. Listening to it again after all these years it remains an accurate portrait of him.

Leah Singer

HUGO BALL

an audio cassette for trish.

HUGO
She Gives Me Love - The Godfathers
Blues from a Gun - Jesus
Deadbeat Club - The B-52's
Backcountry (Live) - G.S.F.
Fall Down - Throwing Muses
GO FISH !
Foxheads - Close Lobsters
'DIS POEM
Twisting - T.M.B.G.
intro./dfds - G.S.F.
Traveling Man - The Woodentops
Instant Club Hit - The Dead Milkmen
Rules & Regulations - Fuzzbox
Preconceptions - Fuzzbox

BALL
Thank God This isn't Cleaveland - Wiscons Insane
On the Way to Oconto - Sigmond Snopek III
Cemetry Gates (Live) - The Smiths
You & a Box of Hankerchiefs - Toy Dolls
Debaser - Pixies
Suburban Holiday - Chuck's a Hippy
Stepping Stone - Sex Pistols
Marry - The Brilliant Corners
Crash - The Primitives
Get into the Groovy - Sonic Youth
Stuart - The Dead Milkmen
Another Reason - G.S.F.
Little Girl - Pulp
Surfin' U.S.A. - Jesus
Deep Down & in Between - Young Fresh Fellows
All the Pretty Girls - The Judys
The GLC Councilor Comments on Punk.

EGGBEATER

eggbeater (a compilation.)

egg side.
She Goes to Finos - Toy Dolls
John the Fisherman - Primus
WRCT God Promo
Just Like Heaven - Dinosaur Jr.
Pink Sunshine - Fuzzbox
Crystal Clear - The Darling Buds
Special One - Ultra Vivid Scene
King of the Mountain - Midnight Oil
Doe; Happiness is a Warm Gun;
Oh!; Hellbound - The Breeders
Rock n' Roll - The Velvet Underground
Rock n' Roll; Sympathy - Jane's Addiction
Loaded - Primal Scream
Hello It's Me - Lou Reed/John Cale

beater side.
Planet Earth - Duran Duran
Backcountry - Green Suade Filth
Christine - Glass Eye
Blues From a Gun - The Jesus & Mary Chain
Been Caught Stealing - Jane's Addiction
Velouria; Allison - Pixies
Idle Gossip - Toy Dolls
Public Service Announcement
Song for a Future Generation - B-52's
Blitzkrieg Bop - The Godfathers
It's Not My Birthday - They Might Be Giants
Groove is in the Heart - Dee Lite

"Hugo Ball: An Audio Cassette for Trish" 1990
This is the first mix tape I made for Trish. I designed this at my job at the Na[val] Base using the lettering machine and copier. I photocopied this image of Hu[go] Ball, one of my favorite Dada artists. The back flap, including the barcode, w[as] photocopied from a Sex Pistols cassette. The final cover was photocopied on[to] a bright flourescent paper.

"Eggbeater (A Compilation)" 1991
Trish and I had a long-distance relationship while we were in college. She was [in] Washington, D.C., and I was in Pittsburgh. I made this while we were freshme[n].

"The College Girl: Round 3 Audio Cassette for Trish" 1993
I was a junior by now and was honing my skills with backward type, aligning typ[e] and more clip art.

Ryan McGinnes[s]

the college girl

an audio cassette for patricia a. goodwin love, ryan j. mcginness

ROUND **3**

the college girl

audio
cassette
for
trish

College side

X-Ray Spex	Oh Bondage, Up Yours!
Shonen Knife	Riding the Rocket
The Buzzcocks	Orgasm Addict
The Wedding Present	Getting Nowhere Fast
Dwarves	Lucky Tonight
Blondie	Call Me
Throwing Muses	Not Too Soon
Schwa	What I Need (is Something)
Milkshakes	Brand New Cadillac
Pixies (Live)	Isla De Encanta
Flock of Seagulls	I Ran
Goo Goo Dolls	Out of Sight
Bee Gees	Tragedy
Bongwater	You Don't Love Me Yet
Thee Headcoats	Cowboys are Square
Babes in Toyland	Bruise Violet
Lush	Nothing Natural

the college girl

Girl side

The Wedding Present	Come Play with Me
Go Gos	We Got the Beat
Sham 69	Borstal Breakout
The Sugarcubes	Hit
Jane's Addiction (Live)	Pigs in Zen
L7	Pretend We're Dead
Stiff Little Fingers	Alternative Ulster
Devo	Whip it
Misfits	Bullet
Sugar	Hoover Dam
Curve	Ten Little Girls
Schwa	Say Zero
Hypno Love Wheel	Antmusic
Chia Pet	Don't You Want Me Baby
The Wedding Present	Thanks

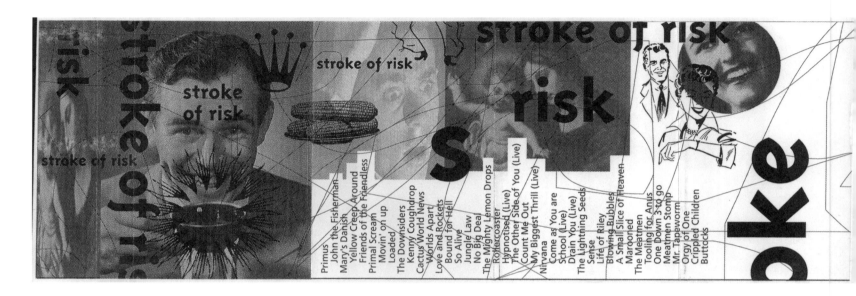

The track list reads:

Primus / John the Fisherman / Mary's Danish / Yellow Creep Around / Friends of the Friendless / Primal Scream / Movin' on up / Loaded / The Downsiders / Kenny Coughdrop / Cactus World News / Worlds Apart / Love and Rockets / Bound for Hell / So Alive / Jungle Law / No Big Deal / The Mighty Lemon Drops / Rollercoaster / Hypnotised (Live) / The Other Side of You (Live) / Count Me Out / My Biggest Thrill (Live) / Nirvana / Come as You are / School (Live) / Drain You (Live) / The Lightning Seeds / Sense / Life of Riley / Blowing Bubbles / A Small Slice of Heaven / Marooned / The Meatmen / Tooling for Anus / One Down 3 to go / Meatmen Stomp / Mr. Tapeworm / Orgy of One / Crippled Children / Buttocks

"Stroke of Risk" 1993

This is just some random mix tape. I made it for myself to listen to in the studio. We can see in this cover that I had learned to use the computer to make scribbles.

"Vomit Here: An Audio Cassette for Trish" 1994

I made this for Trish in the spring of 1994, as we were both graduating from college and getting ready to move to New York City. This piece represents a departure away from line-art drawings towards a concentration on solid iconic forms. I had designed the vomiting person for a senior thesis project for Amtrak (as a joke), and I continued using it for a few years on stickers and t-shirts.

Ryan McGinness

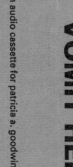

VOMIT HERE

VOMIT HERE

an audio cassette for trish

VOMIT SIDE

The Wedding Present	Give My Love to Kevin
Kajagoogoo	Too Shy
Misfits	I Turned into a Martian
Madonna	Holiday
The Breeders	Cannonball
Material Issue	Valerie Loves Me
Nena	99 Luftballoons
Dwarves	Evil
Naked Eyes	Always Something There...
Ride	Beneath
Butthole Surfers	Tongue
Unknown	Jeanie's Diner
Fudge (live)	Shirts and Skins
Gange of Four	I Love a Man in a Uniform

HERE SIDE

New Order (live)	True Faith
Ministry	Jesus Built My Hotrod
Schwa	Sweet Caroline
Smiths	Sheila Take a Bow
The Ukranians	Bigmouth Strikes Again
Fudge	Girlwish
The Wedding Present	Heather
The Vapors	Turning Japanese
J Church	(Don't Go Back to) Rockville
Sigue Sigue Sputnik	Love Missile F1-110
King Missile	Martin Scorsese
The Cure	Close to Me (Closest Mix)
Talk Talk	Talk Talk

I cannot exactly say when this tape reached me, but it was in the early nineties, certainly pre-1995. It was sent to me in the mail by Jochen Distelmeyer (a German singer-songwriter with the rock-pop band Blumfeld, a sort of a poet) from Hamburg, where he lived, to Cologne, where I was located. Making mix tapes for friends and acquaintances that served as letters/conversation pieces/gifts was a prominent element in a complex practice of his, a way of keeping in touch, exchanging, communicating thoughts and feelings—a practice of excessive yet sensitive articulaton that I cherished and admired and very much loved to share. It also was a kind of mapping out of Jochen's tastes and references to his own developing coming of age as musician and songwriter.

This is one example of a series of cassette tapes that I received from him, a surviving time-capsule of sorts. Most of them were left behind in Cologne, and with some the song list was displaced. His style was writing the list not on the tape but on an extra sheet, often accompanied by a letter. Jochen started touring Germany then, so the stationery for writing out the song list was evidence of him having taken off on his life's journey as an artist. Insofar his mixed tape will let you have a look into a moment of that very process.

Jutta Koether

Hotel garni
Zum Stadttor
Lange Straße 53
3063 Obernkirchen
Tel. 05724/40 16

Joni Mitchell – Strp ot sorrow
Edwyn Collins – A girl like you
Grace Jones – Don't cry – It's only the rhythm
Army of lovers – Cruzified
Mahilia Jackson – Nobody knows
Cass Elliot – Jesus was a Crossmaker
Human League – Human
Ashford & Simpson – Solid
Joyce Sims – Come into my life
Jerry Lee Lewis – High blood pressure
Jerry Lee Lewis – Young blood
Malcolm Mclaren & Lisa – Somethings jumping
PIL – Rise
Manic Street Preachers – Faster
Massive Attack & Tracy Thorn – Protection
David Bowie & Pat Matheny Group – This is not America

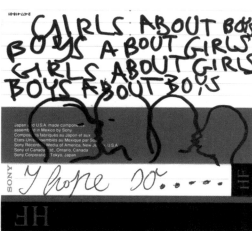

This tape was made for me by Rita Ackermann. Around 1995, Rita and I were dating. When we first met, we made tapes for each other about once a week. We were both dependent on music for inspiration, so the tapes became a quick way for us to communicate our feelings to each other without getting too.... Actually, it wasn't really a quick way to communicate—those tapes took hours to make.

Richard Kern

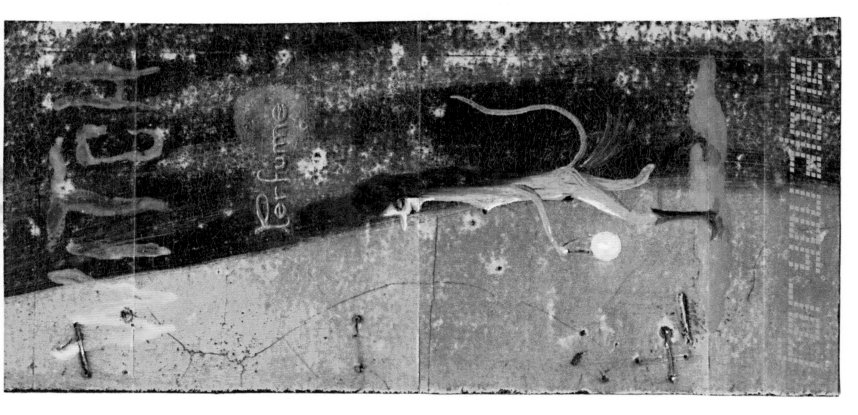

▶

Trisha Donnelly gave me this tape while she was a first-year student in the Yale Sculpture Department. For the cover she collaged a whippet sleeping on a fur pillow onto a patchwork of more fur. The mix has an instrumental by Ritchie Valens and "The Metro" by Berlin.

John Miller

▲

Here is a painting to accompany a tape I made of Halloween-ish songs like "Spooky" and "I Put A Spell On You" and myself trying to write the perfect version of a song called "Witch Perfume." I taped it over a mix that a good friend had made for me of the White Stripes and Chicks on Speed and I don't remember who all. I painted this over the painting he had made for his tape as well... that's his washy moody background that inspired both my painting and my song. That was the last I heard of him. Maybe he thought I was cannibalizing him. Maybe he thinks I shit with Jeffrey Daumer!

Georganne Deen

 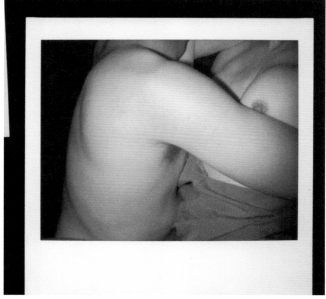

The Cars, *The Cars*, track three
I gave you this record because you kept your Garfield mug even though you threw out all of the photos from when you were a kid. You called me from Berlin and told me that you had fallen in love with me. I was so happy. I had fallen in love with you too. I was nervous, shy. I sent you a message: "Felix, listen to The Cars, *The Cars*, track three on your balcony this morning. I am there with you."

Twisted Sister "We're Not Gonna Take It"
West Side Highway, Halloween. Surrounded by ghosts and goblins on bikes. As they swarmed past us, they began to sing.

Nico, *Chelsea Girls*
We searched the city from the West Side to the East Side, and gave up after leaving a white rose in her apartment. You kissed me under a photo of my cleaved corpse. We ate dinner at midnight in a restaurant nearby, and they played a Nico song— track seven on the record. Later, after you have flown back to Berlin, I listened to the record on headphones while walking under the BQE. Thinking of you, missing you. You called me and repeated the line: "I love you for all the things you are not."

The Bangles, "Hazy Shade Of Winter" and "Eternal Flame"
You heard me humming "Hazy Shade Of Winter" from the other room. You told me that you had bought the record when you quit politics and had listened to that song. One morning, a little later, when I was so low from packing and my troubles in New York, I got a package from you. It had a Bangles CD! I listened to "Hazy Shade" first, and then I listened to "Eternal Flame." I closed my eyes and tried to see your face in my mind.

The Cars, *The Cars*, track one
When did I play this for you? On the first day we met? When I think of this moment, I see sun coming in from the window, and the look of surprise and pleasure on your face when the guitar started. You said this line from track one to me later: "Let the photos be old, let them show what they want."

Felix, I am packing now to come to you, and you have just bought a ticket so that you can come and help me move. When I thank you, you sing "Wild Horses" to me softly. I put on some records: "Here Comes Alex" by Die Töten Hösen, and Iggy Pop's "Now I Wanna Be Your Dog." I am coming to you.

Sue de Beer

Jay Stuckey has been a close friend since the '80s, when we played music in DC, and is one of my favorite artists. Since the beginning of our friendship, we've bonded over '50s/'60s rock 'n' roll and soul, plus the art of mix taping. He gave me this tape—simply covered with the words "sad" and "to feel a little better" along with the creation date—upon the amicable ending of a long engagement. Jay could have easily comforted me with a letter. Instead he made me a mix tape, which perfectly captured the sadness of goodbyes and the determination to channel that pain into creative new beginnings. Jay's covers were usually filled with drawings; what I love about this cover is the use of empty space, which mirrors the emptiness we all feel upon a breakup.

Sharon Cheslow

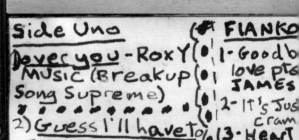

SAD TAPE-STRONG STUFF

UR POSITION NORMAL
A maxell 90

release the sadness 4 more, 3 more, and LEG LIFTS. That's right, Uh-huh, Feel Good

UR POSITION NORMAL
B maxell 90

SAD
3-2-97

Side Uno   FIANKO
1) over you - RoxY   1-Goodb
MUSIC (Breakup   love pts
Song Supreme)   JAMES
2) Guess I'll have to   2-It's Jus
cry cry cry -   cram
JAMES Brown   13-Heart
3) It's easier to cry -   drop-V
Shangri-La's   4-You al
4-HE CRIED-Shangri-   ME-IMP
LA's   5-I'M N
5-CRY CRY CRY-CYNICS   clas
6-CRYING-ROY   6-Here
                                       Laugh
                                       7-How
                                       Blues-
7-CRY TO ME-Solomon   18-His
BURKE   Fla

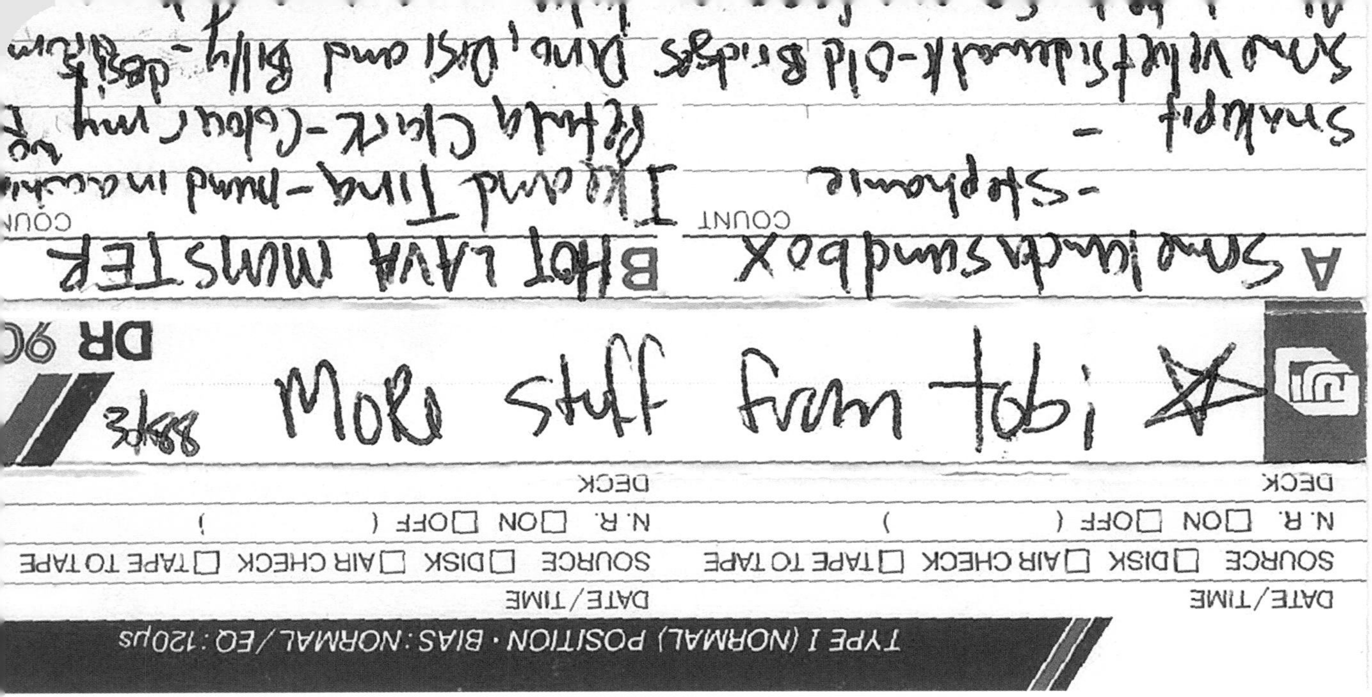

(handwritten cassette inlay, inverted)

DR 90 3/88

More stuff from tobi ✪

A Some kinda Sandbox   **B** HOT LAVA MONSTER
COUNT   COUNT
-Stephanie   I.K. and Ting - Found in cabin
                             Return Check - (when I my be
Snakepit -   Shaking
Snowflake - Old Bridges, Pure, Desi and Billy - desi tom

DECK   DECK
N.R. ☐ ON ☐ OFF ( )   N.R. ☐ ON ☐ OFF ( )
SOURCE ☐ DISK ☐ AIR CHECK ☐ TAPE TO TAPE   SOURCE ☐ DISK ☐ AIR CHECK ☐ TAPE TO TAPE
DATE/TIME   DATE/TIME

TYPE I (NORMAL) POSITION · BIAS: NORMAL/EQ: 120μs

It was embarrassing, back in the '80s, when I was a teen, to admit that the person who most greatly schooled me in rock (and personal/social policitics) was younger than me, but that's how it was. I don't know where I'd be today if it wasn't for the guiding hand of Tobi Vail, but probably not anywhere so lovely as the life I have today. Same goes for Jean Smith. I've learned by far more from these two than anyone else in life, they are my mentors for how to live, what is important, and what matters most, and these tapes were my schoolbooks.

—Slim Moon

DANGEROUS BIRDS, CAT. REV.
COPERNICUS, DAVID THOMAS,
SLITS, UNA MAE CARLISLE;
AU PAIRS, GANG OF 4,
THE OBVIOUS, POISON GIRLS.
SLOW
Ⓐ NO MEANS NO, WANDA
JACKSON, C.C.R, ANNE CLARK

FRIGHTWIG, DREAM.

MOURNING SICKNESS,
5 YEAR PLAN, NICK TOCZEK
MECCA NORMAL -
VARIOUS Conflagrations

Wish We'd Rain...

Romantic Piano /
Burl Ives / Cool Water /Mary Ann /
Requests / Busted /

For Slim from Jean

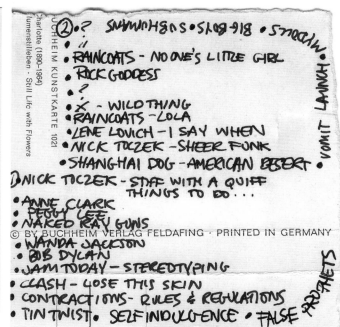

② • ? SUBHUMANS • BIG-BOYS • SUBHUMANS
• "
• RAINCOATS - NO ONE'S LITTLE GIRL
• RICK GODDESS
• ?
• X - WILD THING
• RAINCOATS - LOLA
• LENE LOVICH - I SAY WHEN
• NICK TOCZEK - SHEER FUNK
• SHANGHAI DOG - AMERICAN DESERT
① NICK TOCZEK - STIFF WITH A QUIFF
            THINGS TO DO...
• ANNE CLARK
• PEGGY LEE
• NAKED RAY GUNS
• WANDA JACKSON
• BOB DYLAN
• JAM TODAY - STEREOTYPING
• CLASH - LOSE THIS SKIN
• CONTRACTIONS - RULES & REGULATIONS
• TIN TWIST • SELF INDULGENCE • FALSE PROPHETS
• VOMIT LAUNCH W/DOLLS

BUCHHEIM KUNSTKARTE 1021
Charlotte (1890-1964)
Blumenstilleben · Still Life with Flowers
© BY BUCHHEIM VERLAG FELDAFING · PRINTED IN GERMANY

1   MRX₃ Oxide   MEMOREX   90

2   MRX₃ Oxide   MEMOREX   90

FROM JP & C

N.R.( )
ON/OFF

Some kinda love

Some kinda love

side one
Modern Lovers - she cracked
Wipers - tell public love
Velvet underground - some kinda love
Mary girls - leave me w/ the boy
smash pit - soul like a goat (+ geese)
1993 and the stooges - gimme danger +
Modern lovers - Anne I care about
       Modern world
1/2 Japanese - dream date
Wipers - voices in the rain
side two
Dream Syndicate - when you smile
T Rex - Buick Mackane
Wipers - Doll houses that I am
       somewhat sidewalk - unreleased
Hüsker Dü - something I learned today
Velvet underground - whatever goes on
smash pit - susanville
              miss distrust
                     wait
Mary girls - you must be mad

Side One — to Slim from Tobi 7/87
Rites of spring — In silence / Words Away
Salem 66 • Antietam — Until Now •
The Fall Bombast • thin white rope —
not your fault • throwing muses — America
Soul Asylum — Freaks • Look Blue Go Purple
As does the Sun • beat happening —
the Fall, Look Around, Fourteen, what's
Important?, In Love with you thing, drive g
Fetchin' Bones — so brilliant • the Shan gri
Kansas City • Shop Assistants — Kansas City
I am truly sorry that all of the
last song didn't fit onto this tape

Side two • still to Slim from Tobi
Rites of spring — patience / Velvet Underground
afterhours • Camper Van Beethoven — Peace
and Love • Hüsker Dü — What's goin' on
Kyolving paint Dream — In the afternoon
Patsy Cline — After Midnight • Supreme Cool Being
our advice to you, Don't Panic.
brain thing • Siouxsie — Take me back •
Shop Assistants — I don't wanna be friends
with you, Looking Back, All day long
130/ — Life is full of wonder • Curt Hovland
make everybody happy • Gray Matter
Chutes & Ladders • Raincoats — In Love •
Talulah Gosh — I told you so •

I HAVE SO MANY MIX TAPE STORIES IT'S HARD TO KNOW WHERE TO BEGIN.

I guess I should say I first learned the technology in 1973 when I was living in London and a roommate of mine, Tim Boswood, had the ability to record records onto his cassette deck—it was the first time I had ever seen this. But I personally would have to wait until the end of the '70s before I could afford to have even a used version of this setup. I remember my friend Laurie O'Connell from the band Monitor had a tape deck in her car, and would make tapes with the songs of The Poppy Family or The Shaggs or local bands like The Human Hands. She would listen to this in her car instead of the radio and I was so amazed at the idea that this could be done! She said, "Makes the drive so much more pleasant."

I'm not sure who my first mix tape was for but it's a pretty safe bet I made it for a boy. And I have to admit I became so chronic with always giving boys I was smitten with tapes that I sometimes made some embarrassing mistakes. I made a tape for Nick Cave—can't even remember what I put on there—but I also made a copy of it for myself. Well, at some point for some reason, I gave this copy to Kid Congo Powers. So we're at a barbecue at Kid's house about a year later and Nick Cave is there and Kid plays the tape. "Allison makes this tape for *all* the boys!"

I made tapes for Wim Wenders of girl-group music which is how our mentor/mentee relationship began, that with a detailed song list and an accompanying 35-page letter. I passed tapes back and forth with Kurt Voss, Boyd Rice, and Quentin Tarantino. In fact Quentin made a tape called "True Romance"—he only made 4 copies—one for me, one for Ridley Scott, one for Patricia Arquette, and one for Christian Slater, and they were songs he imagined the characters in the film gave to each other. What made me especially happy was that a song I gave to him on a tape ended up on there: "Last Night In Soho" by Dave Dee Dozy Beaky Mick and Tich.

I received a tape from a man about ten years ago which definitely pushed me from a crush into full-blown love for him. I had given him a tape first after we met, which was all my favorite songs which began with "Stop" by The Moody Blues circa 1965 and ended with "Love" by Victoria Williams. Well, his tape back to me was much more emotional than mine, it was ALL love. The songs promised to never leave, devotion, acceptance, and a real understanding and kindness about who I am and what I meant to him. Some of the gifts on the tape he gave me were "No Matter What" by Badfinger, an insanely beautiful declaration by Richard and Linda Thompson, "A Heart Needs A Home," and "The Day Before You Came" by Abba, which is truly one of the most emotionally charged pop songs ever written. I carried this tape with me everywhere and listened to it constantly. Some four years after he made it for me, I was in NYC working on

"Grace Of My Heart" and got extremely mad at him, and sent it to him in the mail. Yeah I gave it back. Dumped it in the mailbox and sent that right back. And immediately regretted it. I guess I showed him. I'm sure he probably just threw it in the trash, mad at me back, we have never discussed it. Suffice to say, the romantic part of this relationship did not work out, but as we grow older as friends through the ages, all he promised in that tape remains. He is a very devoted friend to me. I have no doubt this tape will be flashing before my ears when my last breath is taken and I pass away onto the next stage.

Damn, how I wish I had that tape back! Not if he remade it—it would not be the same. Because good tapes show their age. You will not make the same tape at 26 that you did at 14 or that you will at 48. My tapes nowadays are usually more in the teacher mode: I recently burned a CD for Eminem which has yet to be sent, cause unlike with mix tapes I find mix CDs much harder to perfect and be satisfied with. I burn from records not from the computer so it takes longer and is hard to get correct. When I send it, and I will, as a fan to him, it will be more of the older pop music self-taught scholar introducing songs he may or may not know.

I also use mix tapes and CDs in my work. The first thing I do when I sit down to write a script is make a tape or CD of the music of the world of the film. Often these songs or songs similar end up in the movie or they inspire something which finds its way to the movie. In *Things Behind The Sun*, Kurt Voss and I used a mix tape between the characters in childhood as a love bond between them, as well as a plot device. It is also the object which propels their healing and the paths they take in their lives. The soundtrack itself was created in part by songs my daughter Tiffany put on a tape for me. Likewise, the soundtrack for *Mi Vida Loca* emerged from the gang kids in Echo Park from tapes they passed amongst themselves and shared with me.

Recently, while teaching at UCSB, in my rock 'n' roll film and soundtrack class, the final project, which was 40% of their grade, was to create the soundtrack of his or her life on a mix tape or CD. I was so enthralled with what I got back—some of these students went so beyond the call: one was her life in the style of a punk rock fanzine; one had hers all done up like a gift in a gift bag because her life had been a gift as far as she was concerned; another student actually created a magazine to go with the CD which was itself encased in a hand-sewn pouch of her own face and brain! Another student made a booklet with pictures, tied by a shoestring and inside the pages there was a story about that very shoestring! Another student did a tie-dyed box set. Another did a Japanese anime story of herself in the third person. The songs on these projects ranged from Jimmie Rodgers to Pink to Def Leppard to Asian folk songs and be-bop jazz and X and Sonic Youth. It was glorious.

I hope the day will never come that I do not find joy in creating and receiving mix tapes and CDs from friends, family, and lovers. It's truly a window into a person's soul and it's the great humanizer. I don't imagine sociopaths make mix tapes, or serial killers, or presidents. Although I still think I might make one for President Clinton. What do you think? Well, maybe after I send this one to Eminem.

Allison Anders

This is a love tape for my husband.

It's actually a graphic of a laughing mouth, shiny red lips, blue tongue, dark maw. It means sweet tastes and hopeless joy with no face. The music is Low, Wedding Present, Helium, Jawbox, Magnetic Fields, Guided By Voices, Takahashi, Brian Eno, David Bowie, Sonic Youth, Blur, Beatles, Dream Syndicate, and Nirvana.

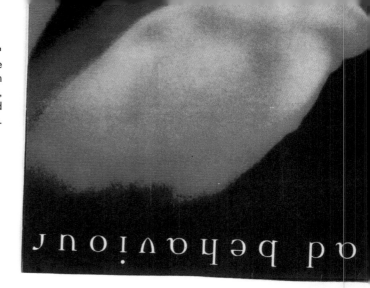

The person who gave me this was like the picture

in that she had small, blunt-nailed fingers and a big sexy mouth. The fingers in this picture are so sensitive with that wrinkly gentle skin. Most of the tape is Queen Latifa, but it's the other side I remember more, because of "Irresistible Bitch" and "Scarlett Pussy" by Prince. The person who gave me this tape was like that too—she was an irresistible bitch!

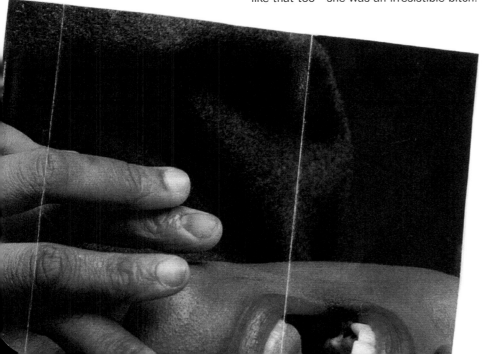

This is dark and strange

partly because of the poor quality of the tape, full of creaks and dark cracks. The music is like artificial light in endless darkness. It has two of the most beautiful songs by the Auteurs', "Bailed Out" and "American Guitars," plus indescribably emotional Mexican music by Califanes. It's so beautiful, like the trembling white faces in silent movies. Sonic Youth ends that section and is followed in a weird segue by Teena Marie and Boney M. The other side the music is like artificial light in the darkness of a crummy club. Is the space woman crying because she is where there's no darkness to light?

I don't know most of the songs on this

and that's good because they are dreamy songs that you want to float past anonymously, changing shapes. I don't know why this doll face is on them, they are like clouds. This tape is like a memory collage made of TV commercials from the sixties and people I saw walking down the street a long time ago. One song is by a man with a rough, sad voice singing "We make the world what it is...by the people we know and the books we read...by the pity we show in the hour of care."

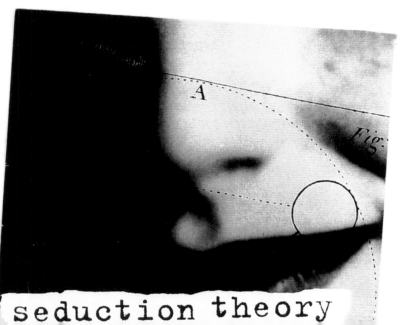

A student made this for me

using a comic strip I did that was up on the Internet. I don't know if the play list has anything to do with it. It starts out with something by Fireman that has piano, water, and space noises, plus, eventually, sex-sounding noises. Then an old woman's Cockney voice comes in saying, "When you least expect it things are gonna be changin'" over and over. I guess that's the therapist. Girl wanders into tunnel of Massive Attack, Garbage, Portishead, Tricky, and John Lydon, clutching handbag muttering "ugly cunt."

Mary Gaitskill

A Spencer Sweeney Mix Tape for Elizabeth Peyton

1. Little Hands—Alexander Spence 2. Fearless—Pink Floyd 3. Not Willing—Moby Grape 4. She Makes Me—Queen 5. Forever Is No Time At All—Pete Townshend 6. Downed—Cheap Trick 7. A Long Way—Queen 8. In Deine Hände—Popul Vuh 9. Ashamed—Emmit Rhodes 10. Harry Flowers—"Performance" soundtrack 11. Time To Get Down—The O'Jays 12. I Don't Know Why—The Rolling Stones 13. Helpless—Neil Young 14. Isn't It A Pity—George Harrison 15. Theo Theodore—Queen 16. Fresh As A Daisy—Emmitt Rhodes 17. Letzte Tage Letzte Nächte—Popul Vuh

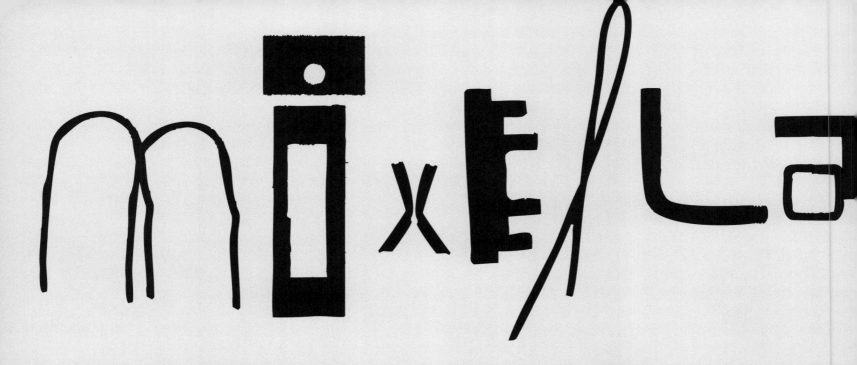

At this point with 10,000 CDs released each day and used record stores brimming over with 99¢ CDs and thrift stores offering CDs and records pennies per pound the best way to really organize it all is to break it down onto tapes. Just plow through the records and record the best bits onto cassette. If you really need to transfer it to CDR, go for it, but remember: you're turning it into a digital format and therefore your ear-heart will tire. Huh? Yeh, you're ear-heart. Dig it: normal bias cassettes rule. (Next to vinyl of course). And it's not a fetish either (well, not entirely...). Vinyl is analog—not a definitive sound wave like digital, which is numeric and perfect transcription. With digital, your brain hears all the information in its numeric perfection. Analog has the mystery arc where cosmos exist, which digital has not reined in. We used to listen to records over and over and each time they would offer something new beacause the ear-heart would respond to new resonations not previously detected. It was like each kiss had a new sensation. Digital format offers one cold kiss. A mere peck. I, for one, grow weary after one taste. Most of your record players have become tabletops for CDs. It's a drag but it's the way of Kali Yuga and who are we, mere mortals, to stop the male-driven technology? These are the "dark ages," but it will ultimately serve to soothe the mother by 2018 thereabouts. Whoa, wait...what am I going on about...oh yes, since your records are in storage, make tapes, mix tapes, and stick them in the tape player in your car. Don't all cars still have cassette functionality? Or has it just gone full on CD?? Oh God.... Anyway, a cassette rocking at normal bias will bring healing analog tones to the ear-heart. Trust me. You won't crash.

T.M.

soundscape...mystic cut-up freeze frame of time. i dont know how it

came to me...or i prefer to pretend not to. a wash...a mixture of sounds,

some i know, others i spend my life searching for titles and matches.

Genevieve Dellinger

se voices screaming in her gut wrenching mirror voice

s blips on a trumpet

heron (this aintre really yr life aint really yr life...)

ects, pushed backwards

fishin yes im going fishin...he'll bet yr life and yr loving wife

hicagothatsmyhometownthatsmyhomefromthehallsofmontezumato
softripoliohwhyamialwaysyearningforteresateresamylove)

l blips , its spacey a bit.... you can't keep me + my family down.

ithink, gett...

layer for 3...

for sure...

gypsy fo

wah w

eee jonaaaaay ro

nn the game

smooth 70's freak*OUT* steppin out in style

coup cuop

panese girls saying merci beaucoup merci beaucoup

(call/ response trigger fuck)

girls jowl toasing chant magick

l backwards (call

the a

ome a long way since i believed in anything, and i come halfway around

the world (ding a ding dang, my dang a-long ling long)

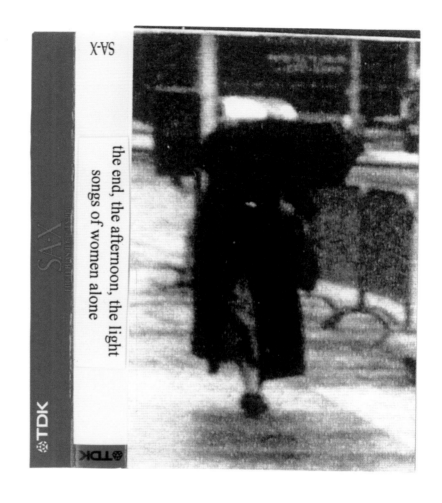

the end, the afternoon, the light
songs of women alone

SA-X

TDK

This is a tape made for women who are alone.

Loren Conners

Alice and Other Tall Women

Side A
Bob Wiseman: No Commotion, Cockroach, Ship at Sea
Souled American: Buck Dancer's Choice
Freedy Johnston: Gina, Little Red-Haired Girl, California Thing,
Tearing Down This Place

Side B
Yo La Tengo: Walking Away From You, Cast A Shadow, Five-Cornered Drone
Drink Me: Grant's Tomb, Ines
The Swales: Always On Your Side
Ringo Starr: Early 1970
The Mekons: Sin City
Elvis Costello: Couldn't Call It Unexpected Number Four

This is an old favorite—a 60-minute tape made for me in the early '90s by my best
friend, Mark Lerner. I was in LA, jobless, floating around. He was in NYC, freshly
married. The cassette couldn't contain all the music. The last song on the b-side ran
out. Mark didn't care. At the time, he and I were both becoming disillusioned with
Elvis Costello, a former idol of ours. In fact, in an accompanying letter, Mark attrib-
uted the song to "Elton Motello," a real insult if you can catch the reference.

Camden Joy

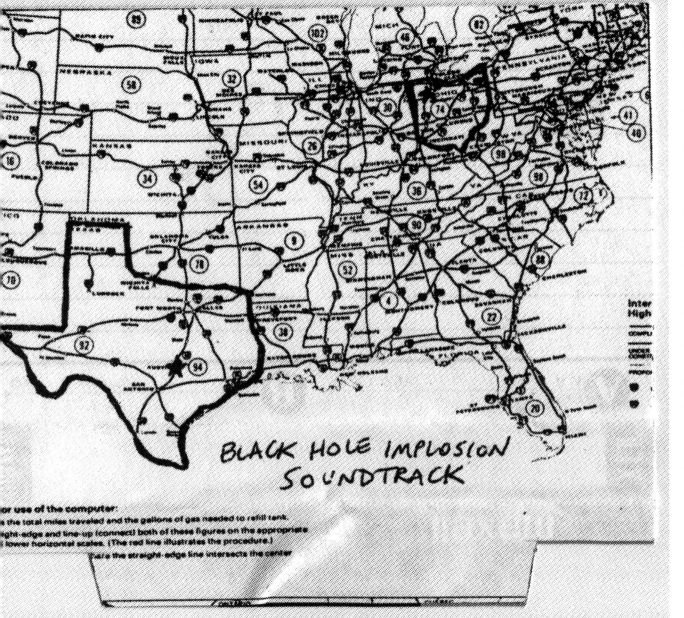

BLACK HOLE IMPLOSION
SOUNDTRACK

or use of the computer:
the total miles traveled and the gallons of gas needed to refill tank.
ight-edge and line-up (connect) both of these figures on the appropriate
lower horizontal scales. (The red line illustrates the procedure.)
ere the straight-edge line intersects the center

For the lack of anything better to do in August '95, I moved from Baltimore to Dallas. En route—though it really wasn't on the way—I dropped my friend and then housemate Dru Bynum off at graduate school in Bowling Green, Ohio. At the time we were living in a two-story rowhouse in an older blue-collar neighborhood of Baltimore that has since become yuppie and gentrified, but we were splitting $415 a month three ways for our proverbial palace. Among friends, the house was affectionately known/derided as "The Black Hole," since the overwhelming inertia of its inhabitants was tragically contagious. For the trip, the all-around stellar human being Vince Griffith—who possesses a record collection known to send full-grown vinyl obscurants weeping to their knees—passed me this tape for the drive, one side of alternating various eras of Texas/Ohio punk, the other of early '90s Austin and '60s Texas garage. Not only did it make a fine driving music, but the Dicks' "Kill From the Heart" is better than trucker speed for keeping you alert when you're crossing the Mississippi from Tennessee to Arkansas at 4 a.m.

Bret McCabe

This is the first tape I made after moving to NYC, specifically the East Village. It was 1992 and I was typically short on funds. To make up for my inability to buy many records I had a habit of recording music off of the radio. I gleefully discovered WFMU's "Cocktail Hour," a one-hour excursion into the then-new lounge craze and started taping all I could get. I was already obsessed with exotica, mambo, and weirdly compelling easy listening music, so it was great to find stuff like this on the radio. I hadn't heard strangeness like this since listening to KNON's *Martian Alien Neon Creature* back in 1980s Dallas on Thursday nights.

Listening to the tape now, even just looking at it, takes me back to my young hopeful desperate life in an apartment filled with furniture culled from the street. I'd paint on found paper while sipping the small luxury that was a cocktail, filled with the crazed energy that a newly married, just-graduated fellow ready to attack the world often is.

It's ten years later now and so many things about that time seem so far away, yet when the Creed Taylor Orchestra kicks in and wafts through the speakers in its stereophonic majesty, the joy and excitement of being alive then is still inside me.

Christian Schumann

the Coctail Hour

Side A

CREE. TAYLOR ORCH - DADDY
DON COSTA - ECHO OF LOVE
ESQUIVEL - KARAOKE
CHARLES CAMIARI - JUNGLE FANTASY
WALTER WANDERLEY TRIO - man + a woman
TERRY SNYDER + TH ALL STARS - BRAZIL
ARTHUR MURRAY - ARTHUR
THE COCTAILS - WHOOPSY-DAISY
DICK HYMAN - MACK THE KNIFE
PERREY + KINGSLEY - STRANGERS IN THE NIGHT
THE GIRLWATCHERS - MUSIC TO WATCH GIRLS BY
LES BAXTER - LUST
THE ISLANDERS - SEA BREEZE
ESQUIVEL and the ZUZU singers - LAZY BONES, SENTIMENTAL JOURNEY
HENRI RENE + ORCH - BAUBLES, BANGLES and BEADS

COMBUSTABLE EDISON - CADILLAC, DEAN ELLIOT - BAUBLES BANGLES and BEADS? (from ZOUNDS WHAT SOUNDS)

SIDE B

WALTER (WENDY) CARLOS - WHATS NEW PUSSYCAT
ETHEL SMITH - NOLA
ESQUIVEL - TICO TICO
HARRY BREWER and his MARIMBAS - SAMBA MACABRE
DUTCH BROADCASTING ORCHESTRA - THEREMIN MUSIC
DICK HARRELL + ORCHESTRA - ROCKET RACKET
BIRB DOMINGUEZ PEPE BLUE RHUMBA
MICHELEMAGNE - BAHIA
RALPH FONT + ORCHESTRA - TABOO
GEORGE WRIGHT - COOL TANGO
ART VAN DAMME QUINTET - ADIOS
MARTIN DENNY - YAYA
ARTHUR LYMAN - LOVE FOR SALE

CONT'D
B GARY MACFARLAND - A HARD DAY'S NIGHT,
STAN GETZ - MANHA DE CARNIVAL
DON ELLIOT - ECHOES OF WEBSTER HALL

I made this cassette, *Oral Surgery Disasters*, in 1995, the night before I was getting a dental implant for a tooth I lost that broke on a plane flight after a root canal that was not crowned properly. The tooth then had to be extracted totally. I was warned that the surgery would take up to 90 minutes, and they would be drilling into my jawbone and inserting a titanium bolt to put a new crown on top of.

I don't like going to the dentist to begin with, so I thought I'd make a cassette to distract me from the drilling that was going to be going on in my head. The sounds and tempo (and even some lyrics) of the songs were meticulously picked (as well as the sequence) to ease the whole situation, and I left *no* blank space between songs to drown out every last bit of gnarly noise.

I was so nervous they gave me some laughing gas to calm me down just before the surgery, but indeed I was awake. The cassette was so perfect, and I was getting so into listening to it during the surgery, I actually kicked the table of tools in front of me while getting into the music a little too enthusiastically. When they told me they were done and my cassette had not finished, I said, "Are you sure?"

Glen E. Friedman

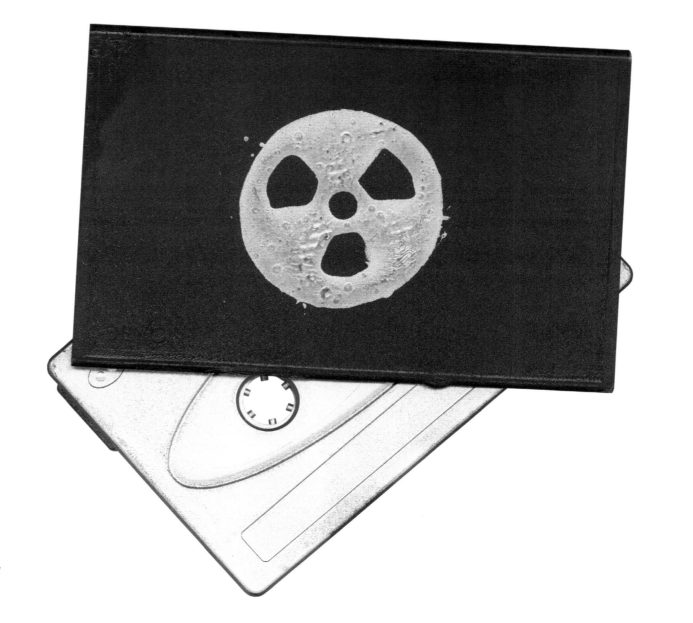

DJ Spooky

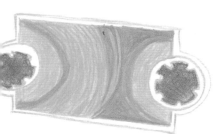

I made this tape in the summer of 2002 for my best friend who was living in New York at the time. We've been best friends since high school, but haven't lived in the same city for 10 years. We've always sent mixed tapes back and forth to keep each other up to date on what we're listening to.

I put some late '70s/early '80s pop, a little English folk rock, and some '60s stuff on it as well as some other music I refer to as Showcore: Klaus Nomi, GTOs, Sparks, and Susan Tyrrell from the soundtrack of *Forbidden Zone* (1980).

These songs have a specific crazy performance element to them. Theatrical or operatic, hard-core show tunes. I used to be very close to Susan Tyrrell. She's an Academy Award–nominated actress from the '70s. She's also a pirate and guru. She lived up the street from me in Echo Park, and I would bring her beer and cigarettes in exchange for acting lessons.

Jade Gordon

GOODBYE'S TOO GOOD A WORD
Five Byproducts of a Break-Up Mix

1. A newfound appreciation for the sentimentality of Black Flag
I never thought I'd find myself tearing up over "Hot Child in the City" or X, but even the happy songs make me cry. I think if they were exclusively "break-up" songs it would lose some of its potency. Probably because the extended end of our relationship was analogously decorated with those intense highs as well as lows, and this tape was gifted to me in final stages of that drawn-out dénouement.

2. New dance moves
The last time I was cutting a rug at a party and I heard those haunting opening bars to "Temptation" I invented a new move that incorporated wiping my nose and eyes. Talk about sexy.

3. Hiding places
I had to dig the tape out of the place I've most recently hidden it from myself so that I could do this project (kitchen pantry, behind those yummy canned weenies). If I leave it lying around too much it always ends up back in my tape deck and I end up back in tears. So it's been inside my vacuum cleaner, my spare tire compartment, summer storage in the pockets of my winter coats, in my old stereo (which doesn't work and requires pliers for ejection)…

4. Communication through 443 feet of Magnetized Plastic
Steve wouldn't speak with me most of the summer after he gave me this. For months, this tape was the only voice I heard from someone who taught me how to love (even if only for the sake of that single relationship). So a piece of black plastic sparsely decorated with white-out is somehow the most significant symbol of that nauseatingly painful deletion from "in love" to "love."

5. An excuse to see Steve
Tonight, after watching a Rex Smith movie with Gaby and Jade (which coincidentally had "You Take My Breath Away" in the soundtrack), I went over to Steve's and sobbed to the music while he helped me figure out the tracks I didn't know. He made me peppermint tea and I told him how he had ruined every song on the tape for me, since now they all make me cry. He corrected me, telling me that he had actually vitalized them for me by infusing them with meaning. Maybe he was right.

Daniella Meeker

The following playlist for "Indians Jumpin' On Fire" is for a collection of Mardi Gras Indian music that's one of 13 mixes I've assembled of Mardi Gras music from New Orleans. There isn't any cover design but any image of a Wild Indian will do. This is the shit, believe me! Tracks are mostly from locally released albums, singles, or cassettes.

Mardi Gras Collection
Volume Five
Indians Jumpin' On Fire!
Wild Indians of Mardi Gras, Part 2

1. Wild Tchoupitoulas: "Indian Red" (Antilles, 1975)
2. Wild Apaches: "Indians Jumpin' On Fire" (SONO, 1997)
3. Indians of the Nation: "Early in the Morning" (Ch'Ching, 1999)
4. Flaming Arrows: "Sew, Sew" (Mardi Gras, 1997)
5. Young Guardians of the Flame: "Big Chief Where Are You" (First Tribe, 1998)
6. Wild Tchoupitoulas: "Hey Hey (Indians Comin')" (Antilles, 1975)
7. Guardians of the Flame: "Two-Way-Pocky-Way" (Candid, 1991)
8. Golden Eagles: "Hoon Na Day"/"Monk's Dream" (Rounder, 1988)
9. Flaming Arrows: "Here Come the Indians Now" (Mardi Gras, 1997)
10. Bayou Renegades: "Old Time Indian" (Kolab, 1992)
11. Guardians of the Flame: "Shallow Water" (Candid, 1991)
12. 9th Ward Hunters & ReBirth Brass Band: "Shoe Fly" (GPG, 1992)
13 Indians of the Nation: "No No No" (Ch'Ching, 1999)
14. Young Guardians of the Flame: "Indian Red" (First Tribe, 1998)

John Sinclair

In high school, I would drive around for any reason at all to smoke and listen to this tape.

Kate Spade

maxell. XLII 90

POSITION · IEC TYPE II · HIGH[CrO₂]

THE COACH HOUSE

A DATE . . N.R. ☐ YES ☐ NO	**B** DATE . . N.R. ☐ YES ☐ NO
PABLO PICASSO (MODERN LOVERS), BOY WITH PERPETUAL NERVOUSNESS (THE FEELIES), HEROIN (VELVET UNDERGROUND) RUNAWAYS (XTC), S.F. NIGHTS (ERIC BURDON : THE ANIMALS), HELLO IT'S ME (TODD RUNDGREN) I GO TO RIO (PABLO CRUISE), BETH (KISS), UP ON THE SUN (MEAT PUPPETS), BLANK GENERATION (RICHARD HELL & THE VOIDOIDS), TV EYE (THE STOOGES) SHE'S SO MODERN (BOOMTOWN RATS) HAPPY DAY (TALKING HEADS) WATCHING THE DETECTIVES (ELVIS COSTELLO)	SEE NO EVIL (TELEVISION), HOSPITAL (MODERN LOVERS), ERUPTION (VAN HALEN), SAFE EUROPEAN HOME (CLASH) TEENAGE KICKS (UNDERTONES), LEXICON DEVIL (THE GERMS), WAITRESS IN THE SKY (THE REPLACEMENTS), SEARCH (MINUTEMEN) UNCONTROLLABLE URGE (DEVO), WASTED LIFE (STIFF LITTLE FINGERS), I CONFESS (ENGLISH BEAT), THAT'S NOT ME (BEACH BOYS), LIVING IN THE PAST (JETHRO TULL), TATTOOED LOVE BOYS (PRETENDERS)

A | **B**

Most of this music is from late high school through early college. It was a time in Arizona when a small group of us were skateboarding in empty swimming pools with the car speakers blasting in the background. It was 120 degrees out. Those were the days. The name of this mix tape, *The Coach House*, is after a bar in old Scottsdale with Christmas decorations up all year. It was the kind of place you went to when you were 18 or 19.

Andy Spade

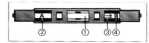

① Non-abrasive head cleaning leader tape.
② Indicates A or B side ready to play.
③ Arrows indicate direction of tape travel.
④ 5-second cueing line.

for B side
Breakout lug
for A side

This old R-R tape that I began recording in Copenhagen in 1960 ain't so much a mix as a sign of things to come, with its great clash of Kagel and Valens, Pierre Henry, and Don & Phil E. And does anyone else still remember "Do-Do-Do?"

Tony Conrad

The Everly Brothers' Best
(copied from Peter's Tape)
Bye Bye Love
I Wonder If I Care As Much
Wake Up Little Suzie
Maybe Tomorrow
This Little Girl of Mine
Should We Tell Him
All I Have to do Is Dream
Claudette
Bird Dog
Devoted to You
Problems
Love of My Life
Poor Jenny
Cathy's Clown

Music by Henry, Philippot from Second Panorama
de Musique Concrete
Ducretet Thompson DUC 2001
(including parts of "Symphonie pour un Homme seul"
played at 78 r.p.m)

Boogie Woogie Prayer (parts I & II)   on Colu
  Meade Lux Lewis, Pete Johnson, Albert Ammons,
Do-Do-Do (from "Oh Kay.")   on Victor
  Geo. Olsen & his Music, vocal: Bob Borger, Frank Fre...
Give Your Mamma One Smile (Bill Broonzy)   on Vic...
  Lil Green
My Mellow Man (Willie Broonzy)   (incomple
  Lil Green   on Vict. Bluebird

Ritchie Valens   Delofi   DFL

That's My Little Suzie
In a Turkish Town
Come On, Let's Go
Donna
Boney-Maronie (Williams)
Ooh, My Head
La Bamba (Adapted-Valens)
Bluebirds Over the Mountain (Hickey)
Hi-Tone (Hazan)
Framed (Leiber-Stoller)
We Belong Together (Carr-Mitchell)

All by 17-y
Valens, e...
where, in...
He is from
Fernando,

TOP 14 OF 1977

1. WHEN I NEED YOU Leo Sayer
2. HOTEL CALIFORNIA The Eagles
3. WHO DONE IT Tavares
4. SIR DUKE Stevie Wonder
5. I'M YOUR BOOGIE MAN K. C. and The Sunshine Band
6. SOVERN NIGHTS Glen Campbell
7. YOU GOT TO GIVE IT UP Marvin Gaye
8. I'M SO INTO YOU The Atlantic Rhythm Section
9. COULDN'T GET IT RIGHT Climax Blues Band
10. RIGHT TIME OF THE NIGHT Jennifer Warnes
11. DREAMS Fleetwood Mac
12. THE THING WE DO FOR LOVE 10CC
13. THEME FROM ROCKY Bill County
14. I GOT LOVE ON MY MIND Natalie Cole

TOP 14 OF 1977

1. WHEN I NEED YOU Leo Sayer
2. HOTEL CALIFORNIA The Eagles
3. WHO DONE IT Tavares
4. SIR DUKE Stevie Wonder
5. I'M YOUR BOOGIE MAN K. C. and The Sunshine Band
6. SOVERN NIGHTS Glen Campbell
7. YOU GOT TO GIVE IT UP Marvin Gaye
8. I'M SO INTO YOU The Atlantic Rhythm Section
9. COULDN'T GET IT RIGHT Climax Blues Band
10. RIGHT TIME OF THE NIGHT Jennifer Warnes
11. DREAMS Fleetwood Mac
12. THE THINGS WE DO FOR LOVE 10CC
13. THEME FROM ROCKY Bill County
14. I GOT LOVE ON MY MIND Natalie Cole

Christopher Knowles

this page
9,712, 1999
The number 9,712 is the sum playing time of all cassettes in the painting.

Christian Schumann

opposite
Moebius Loop, 1994
cassette tapes, nylon ties
24 x 84 x 240 in.

Christian Marclay

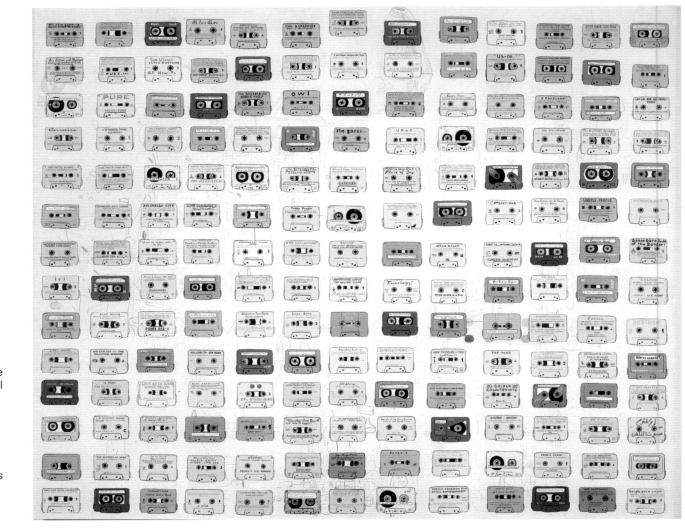

Big Mix For Big Nose
A mix tape for my father, circa 1987

Side 1
Vince Guaraldi—*Peanuts* theme
Beatles
Stevie Wonder—Living For The City
Rolling Stones
Badbrains
Syd Barrett
Velvet Underground—Heroin
Talking Heads

Side 2
Cream—*Disraeli Gears*
Minutemen—*Doublenickles On The Dime*
(excerpts)

opposite: *19 Pink Jap Cass*, 2000

Tom Sachs

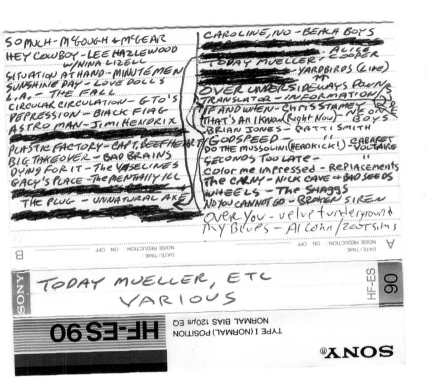

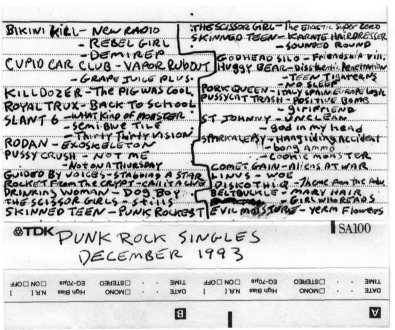

I just located the mix tape I talked about—the one called 'H.C.' Here it is, in all its stark minimalist glory.

Thurston Moore

CONTRIBUTORS

Lasse Marhaug is an avant-garde design artist and noise musician from Norway. His mix tape was a gift from fellow Norwegian **Kjell Runar Jenssen**, a drummer and percussionist in Motorpsycho.

Pat Griffin is a chef based in Oregon.

Ahmet Zappa is an actor and musician based in Los Angeles.

Karen Constance a.k.a. **Karen Lollypop** is a visual artist and avant-garde noise musician from the UK who has issued recordings as Smack Music 7 and the Polly Shang Kuan Band. Her mix tape was made for an ex-Polly Shang Kuan Band member, but she never gave it to her.

Mike Watt is a founding member of San Pedro, California, punk revolutionaries the Minutemen. Amongst other activities he records and tours a perpetual series of punk operas as well as handling bass duties in the reignited Iggy & The Stooges. His mix tape was a gift from **Steven Drozd** from the Flaming Lips.

Glen E. Friedman is a photographer who has shot the punk, hardcore, skate, and hip-hop scenes from the early 1980s onward. His work has appeared on record sleeves for Run DMC, LL Cool J, Ice-T, and Black Flag. His mix tapes came from **Pushead** a.k.a. **Brian Schroeder**, one of the most distinguished artists and writers to come out of the first generation USA hardcore scene. His work has appeared on T-shirts, posters, and record sleeves for countless artists, including Necros, Metallica, The Misfits, Dr. Octagon, and Corrosion of Conformity.

Cynthia Connolly is a photographer who helped establish Dischord Records as a perennial label for local and progressive music in the Washington, D.C. area. Since taking leave she has focused on travel and new eye documentation exhibiting her work most recently in the acclaimed Beautiful Losers group show at the Yerba Buena Center for the Arts in San Francisco in 2004.

Dean Wareham, Damon Krukowski & Naomi Yang started the band Galaxie 500 in 1987 and immediately resonated with the underground rock scene from their hometown of Boston to distant lands. They ended in 1991, with Dean continuing with his rock group Luna, and Damon and Naomi working as a duo.

Tom Greenwood resides amongst the Portland, Oregon mysterioso nexus as a musician and visual artist, infamous for creating the shapeshifting free rock ensemble Jackie O Motherfucker.

David Choe is a drummer and painter. His work has been described as "beautifully disturbing" by *Vice* magazine.

Matias Viegener is a writer and critic based in Los Angeles. His criticism appears in the anthologies *Queer Looks: Lesbian & Gay Experimental Media* (Routledge), and *Camp Grounds: Gay & Lesbian Style* (U Mass). He has published fiction in the anthologies *Men on Men 3*, *Sundays at Seven*, *Dear World*, *Abjects*, and *Discontents*, edited by Dennis Cooper. He is the editor and co-translator of Georges Batailles' *The Trial of Gilles de Rais*. He has most recently published fiction and criticism in such magazines as *Bomb*, *Artforum*, *Art Issues*, and *Semiotext(e)*.

Lili Dwight is the mother of Addison Coley and Hudson Coley. She is a bright star in the eyes of all who know her. Her mix tapes are gifts from her beloved **Byron Coley**, a writer and archivist of all that is spirited and free.

Mac McCaughan started the Raleigh, North Carolina bands Superchunk and Portastatic and runs the independent record label Merge. His mix tape was a gift from **Jonathan Marx**, who founded the band Lambchop.

Dodie Bellamy is a radical female poet/writer/essayist who in one swoop decimated and furthered experimental prose/poetry with the sensational *Cunt Ups* (Soft Skull). Her most recent book is *Pink Steam* (Suspect Thoughts).

Dan Graham is seen as one of the most significant artists from the 1960s/70s New York City conceptual art scene whose work continues to astound. His essays on pop music have been published in *Crawdaddy* and *Artforum*. His writings have been collected in the anthologies *Rock My Religion* (MIT) and *Two-Way Mirror Power* (MIT).

William Winant is a premier new music percussionist who has worked with John Cage, Iannis Xenakis, Yo-Yo Ma, Mr. Bungle, and others. **John Zorn** is a composer, saxophonist, and bandleader, who is responsible for bringing together seemingly opposing musical genres in the last twenty years.

Jim O'Rourke is a musician/composer residing in the dark byways of Brooklyn, New York. He has worked in collaboration with Takehisa Kosugi and the Merce Cunningham Dance Company as well as John Zorn, Derek Bailey, Merzbow, Loren Connors, and Ikue Mori. He has produced and performed with Sonic Youth and Wilco, as well as maintaining an unbeatable reputation as a karaoke kingpin.

Leah Singer is an artist/filmmaker living in New York City. She has published the artist newsprint book *Copy*, a collection of silhouette images, which she has extended to mainstream ad work. Her mix tape is a gift from her husband and collaborator **Lee Ranaldo** of the experimental rock quintet Sonic Youth.

Ryan McGinness is an artist/designer who came straight out of skate culture and landed solid into the contemporary art world. He published the best seller *Flatnessisgod* in 1999.

Jutta Koether is an artist from Cologne, Germany, living, working and teaching in New York City. She has performed and showed her paintings and installations internationally, regularly showing in New York with the Pat Hearn Gallery. She is currently represented by Galerie Daniel Buchholz in Cologne. Her mix tape was a gift from **Jochen Distelmeyer**, singer of Blumfeld, a legendary independent rock band from Hamburg, Germany.

Richard Kern has lived and worked in New York City since 1979. In the 80s he produced a series of short films that are recognized as the central works of the movement known as the Cinema of Transgression. In the 90s he switched to photography full time and occasionally directed music videos for bands like Sonic Youth and Marilyn Manson. A number of books have been published of his work, most notoriously *New York Girls* (Taschen).

Rita Ackermann is a New York City artist, originally from Hungary, who entranced everyone living below Houston Street during the 1990s with her drawings and paintings of impetuous young females. She has since become a high profile gallery artist and a mesmerizing performer with the groups Angelblood, Diadal, and others.

John Miller is an artist and essayist living in New York City with his family. He has exhibited internationally over the last thirty years, predominantly in the U.S. and mainland Europe. In the mid 80s he worked as the U.S. editor of the British magazine *Artscribe*. He now contributes regularly to the Berlin-based journal *Texte zur Kunst*.

Trisha Donnelly is an artist, originally from San Francisco, now living in Los Angeles. Her 2002 show at Casey Kaplan gallery in New York City—where she exhibited a stirring mix of performance, DVD projection and photography—introduced her as a vital new presence in the art world.

Georganne Deen is an artist and poet living in Los Angeles, California, originally from the wilds of Fort Worth, Texas. Her work is a melange of beauty, both sensual and hideous, which has graced album covers as well as an international list of gallery exhibits. Her poetry is collected in *Season of the Western Witch* published by Viggo Mortensen's Percival Press.

Sue de Beer is a Berlin-based artist known for her startling depictions of people which challenge the notions of natural and normal. Her work is exhibited regularly around the world, and is in the collections of several major institutions.

Sharon Cheslow is a sound artist originally from Washington, D.C., where in the early 1980s she was a founding member of the all-girl rock band Chalk Circle. She was instrumental in the pro-feminist activities of the early-1990s Riot Grrl community. For more than a decade she has published the radical music fanzine *Interrobang* and the Decomposition distribution outlet for experimental music as well as maintaining a site documenting female artists of the early punk and experimental scene of the 1970s/80s. Her mix tape is from **Jay Stuckey**, a visual artist living and working in Los Angeles.

Slim Moon is a musician and proprietor of the Kill Rock Stars label in Olympia, Washington. His mix tapes are from **Tobi Vail**, a musician also from Olympia, who has been instrumental in presenting ideas and actions through punk rock. An original voice of the new feminist Riot Grrl collective, she has created music with Bikini Kill, The Frumpies, and others.

Allison Anders is a deeply personal filmmaker who has used her own experience to make bittersweet and realistic studies of women coming of age amid tough social conditions.

Mary Gaitskill is the author of *Bad Behavior* (Vintage), *Because They Wanted To* (Simon & Schuster), and *Two Girls Fat and Thin* (Simon & Schuster).

Spencer Sweeney is an artist living in New York City who, when not covering a gallery floor-to-ceiling in a paper hurricane of radical rock 'n' roll pen drawings, is spinning vinyl as the city's best headtripping DJ.

Elizabeth Peyton is a painter who caught the art world's eye in a sweet and seductive moment in the mid-1990s. Her work is a heartbeat rendering of pop music lads and other such creatures with an underlying sense of desire and privacy.

Genevieve Delliger is a musician/artist who has recorded and performed with the roving vagabond experimentalist combo Jackie O Motherfucker. She has published a collaborative book of poetry with Matthew Wascovich from Slow Toe Publications.

Loren Connors is a guitarist/artist/poet working since the early 1970s. He has an extensive catalogue of slow, subterranean blues, starting with the now-infamous Unaccompanied Acoustic Guitar Improvisations series, self-released on the Dagget label. In the early 1980s, he recorded a plethora of small pressing LPs under the St. Joan imprint. He ceased playing to concentrate on haiku and painting. In 1988 he returned to playing and recording anew and has become one of the most significant guitar improvisers working in the last twenty years.

Camden Joy is a self-proclaimed pop fabulist who has written one of the great rock 'n' roll novels of the last century, *Boy Island* (Morrow/Harper Collins) as well as the acclaimed *The Last Rock Star Book or Liz Phair, A Rant* (Verse Chorus Press).

Bret McCabe is a music writer and critic based in Baltimore, Maryland.

Christian Schumann is a California-based artist whose predominately cartoonlike collage and paintings engage the theme-park horrors of contemporary existence.

DJ Spooky a.k.a. **That Subliminal Kid** has been an active force on the multidynamic art/music/information exploration and remix-theory front since being first identified as one of the true super-post-modern DJ pioneers.

Jade Gordon is a performer and musician based in Los Angeles.

Daniella Meeker is a Ph.D. candidate in Computation and Neural Systems at Caltech.

John Sinclair is a poet who helped found the Detroit Artists' Workshop and subsequently the Artists' Workshop Press in 1964. In 1967 he helped organize Trans-love Energies Unlimited, a "total cooperative tribal living and working commune" which, amongst other things, served as a cooperative booking agency and management for rock groups The MC5, The Stooges and The UP. In November 1968, deeply influenced by the Black Panthers, Sinclair helped found the White Panther Party. In July 1969, he was sentenced to prison for ten years for possession of two marijuana cigarettes. While incarcerated he wrote *Guitar Army* (Douglas/World). His prolific writings appeared in numerous publications and made him a national symbol. Fifteen thousand people attended the Free John Now Rally headlined by John Lennon and Yoko Ono. Three days later Sinclair was released. He continues to write poetry and has had a long run as a blues DJ on WWOZ in New Orleans.

Kate Spade is an award-winning accessories designer, and the author of three books on modern etiquette. Her iconic brand includes shoes, home and bedding, and, recently, music.

Andy Spade is a co-founder of Kate Spade handbags, and the president and creative director of Jack Spade, a line of hip utilitarian men's bags and accessories.

Tony Conrad is an avant-garde video artist, experimental filmmaker, musician, composer, sound artist, teacher, and writer. Along with John Cale, Angus MacLise, La Monte Young, and Marian Zazeela, he was a co-founder of the Theater of Eternal Music, which utilized non-Western musical forms and sustained sound to produce dream music. Their collective work *Day of Niagara* is one of the earliest examples of minimalist composition. *The Flicker* is considered a key early work of the structural film movement. He has composed more than a dozen audio works with special scales and tuning for solo amplified violin with amplified strings. He continues to teach at the Department of Media Study at SUNY Buffalo.

Christopher Knowles is an autistic poet. His poetry was discovered by Robert Wilson and used for the avant-garde minimalist Phillip Glass' opera *Einstein on the Beach*. Knowles has produced very little solo work. *Typings* (a volume of poetry) received good notices. Otherwise, he has continued to collaborate with Robert Wilson, and Wilson has used Knowles's texts in many of his operas.

Christian Marclay is an artist and musician living and working in New York City since the late 70s. His turntable performance pieces were developed alongside the DJ culture revolution and offered a perspective wholly new and other. His gallery and museum work incorporates his devotion to the record, the record player and sound and film sampling as sense-memory issues and action.

Tom Sachs is a New York-based artist who assembles familiar objects into surprising and often shocking forms in a medium he calls bricolage. His works include the "Chanel Guillotine," the "Prada Toilet," and a 4,000-square-foot Le Corbusier-inspired installation called "Nutsy's."

ACKNOWLEDGMENTS

In loving memory of the audiocassette tape.

Editor: Thurston Moore
Rizzoli/Universe Editor: Eva Prinz
Concept & Design: Andrew Prinz at the Simultaneous Workshop
Contributing Editors: Dean Wareham and Jon Guzik
Production Manager: Anet Sirna-Bruder

Many thanks to the following people, without whom, this book could not have come together:
Allied Cultural Prosthetics, Ahmet Zappa, Allison Anders, Andy Spade, Anet Sirna-Bruder, Brian Lightbody, Byron Coley, Charles Miers, Chris Elliot, Christian Marclay, Christian Schumann, Christopher Knowles, Cynthia Connolly, Damon Krukowski, Dan Graham, David Berman, David Choe, Dean Wareham, Dodie Bellamy, Dylan Nyoukis, DJ Spooky, Elizabeth Peyton, Gavin Brown, Genevieve Delliger, Georganne Deen, Glen E. Friedman, Ilaria Urbinati, Jason Lee, Jean Smith, Jim O'Rourke, John Zorn, John Miller, John Sinclair, Jon Guzik, Jutta Koether, Karen Lollypop, Kate Spade, Kim Gordon, Lasse Marhaug, Leah Singer, Lili Dwight, Loren Connors, Lydia Lunch, Mac McCaughan, Mary Gaitskill, Matias Viegener, Michael Gira, Mike Watt, Naomi Yang, Neil Strauss, Niki Elliot, Oberon Sinclair, Pat Griffin, Pete Kember, Peter Halley, Richard Kern, Richard Kostelanetz, Rita Ackermann, Ryan McGinness, Slim Moon, Sharon Cheslow, Spencer Sweeney, Steven Drozd, Sue de Beer and Tom Sachs.

Also thanks to: Jacquie Byrnes, John Deen, Julie Di Filippo, Susan Fensten, Caitlin Leffel, Susan Lotas, Ellen Nidy, Gerard Nudo, Kiki Sinclair and Mike Slack.

Thank you: Maxell, Sony, TDK, Memorex, Philips, Technics, BASF, Denon, Scotch, and 3M.

Original tape collage by contributors noted, except:
Collage and illustrations on page opposite of table of contents, on page 6 and page 7 by Brian Lightbody, courtesy of the artist.
Page 87, Christian Marclay, *Moebius Loop*, 1994, (sculpture) cassette tapes, nylon ties, 24 x 84 x 240 inches, courtesy of Paula Cooper Gallery, New York.
Page 84, Christopher Knowles, *Untitled (Top of 14 of 1977)*, 1977, typing on paper, 2 parts, each 11 x 8 $^1/_2$ inches, (CK 039) courtesy of the artist and Gavin Brown's Enterprise, New York.
Page 89, Tom Sachs, *2000 19 Pink Jap Cass*, courtesy of Baldwin Gallery and Allied Cultural Prosthetics, New York.